Contents

Almost a Hero

The experiences of a young Scot in the Royal Marines
in the Second World War

By

Alex Clark

With a foreword by His Royal Highness,
The Prince Philip, Duke of Edinburgh, K.G., K.T.

*To
Alistair*

Best wishes

Alex. Clark

24/09/01

Gopher Publishers: www.gopherpublishers.com

ISBN 90-76249-96-2
404^e print, augustus 2001

Copies can be ordered via the Internet: www.gopherpublishers.com
or from
Gopher Publishers UK
14 Harrow Inn Close
Elgin
IV30 1BP
Tel. +44 (0) 1343 550 245
Fax. +44 (0) 1343 550 781

Photographs and Illustrations

Foreword

It so happens that I was serving with the Mediterranean Fleet in 1941 during the Battle of Crete and the subsequent evacuation of our forces from the island. Unfortunately, the author was one of the unlucky ones who we failed to get off the island. The battle against the Luftwaffe, while the evacuation was going on, was quite dramatic and several ships were sunk including HMS Kelly, which was commanded at the time by my uncle, Lord Mountbatten.

The Fleet and the survivors returned to Alexandria and we got on with the war. It was only after reading this account that I discovered what had happened to those who could not be evacuated. It is a grim story, although parts of it are lightened by the author's sense of humour. I am glad that it has been recorded for the benefit of the author's family and friends as well as for future historians.

It is a quirk of fate that the author now lives in Ballater, not far from Balmoral and that we happened to meet some years ago in a fishing hut beside Loch Muick. But that is another story.

His Royal Highness, The Prince Philip,
Duke of Edinburgh, K.G., K.T.,

Author's Introduction

I have used the two words Almost and Hero in the title for two reasons.

The first word, Almost, describes a number of occasions during my five years of war when something very important almost happened. It was a period that covered my training in the Royal Marines, the Battle of Crete, where I was captured, and my four years in German Prisoner-of-War camps.

The second word, Hero, was inspired by a cutting from a Glasgow evening newspaper of 1941. At that time I was doing hard labour in a stone quarry in a POW camp in the Black Mountains in Czechoslovakia. Many other words might have described my incarceration and my activities – strenuous, exhausting, starving, humiliating, soul destroying, even stoic but not heroic. When the very first letter from my Mum arrived in our Prison Camp, the cutting fell out. It had a photograph of me under the heading, 'Crete Hero Missing', with a brief statement that I had been captured in the Battle of Crete. I learned later that the reporter was a friend and neighbour. It was a good topical and local article but, for all he knew, I might have only been captured after a lengthy and lung bursting chase by the Germans. I was looking for a title for this book - one that might attract attention. The word hero always attracts attention but I had no doubt that the description in the newspaper could not be applied to me. I looked it up in the dictionary just in case there was a humorous and light-hearted definition. There was none, so I looked up a similar word, 'stoic'. The definition was: 'austere impassivity; uncomplaining fortitude in suffering'. While the word stoic might possibly be applied to my POW experience, the word heroic, as applied to my Crete experience, definitely needs the qualifying 'Almost'. I'll leave it as the title.

My first aim in writing was to leave to my family some record of what life was like for one of their grandparents in this twentieth century. In particular I have in mind my grandchildren and my great grandchildren, although the latter are as yet unborn. When I was a laddie at school, I visited my Grandma Robertson most days. She was ill and needed my Mum's attention. She talked to me of her childhood in Perthshire, matters that my own parents perhaps did not even know. She seemed to me a very wise person and I confided in her many things that bothered me. Not world shattering matters but very important matters to a schoolboy. An example comes to mind. I went to a Grammar school but Dad could not afford the pocket money that most of the boys had. I would not have upset my Dad for all the tea in China because I knew how very hard up we were. I was telling my Grandma about a very rich chum at school who was given a half-crown (a lot of money in those days) for pocket money every week. Dad could not afford that. She took out her purse and gave me a half-crown piece. She said: "Now, Alex, you are a clever wee laddie and just as good as your rich chum. You put that half crown in your top pocket where you won't see it all the time. Don't ever spend it and you too will always have a half-crown pocket money like your rich friend." I thought that even Solomon did not have the wisdom of my old Grandma whom I loved so much.

The reason I mention the story about my Grandma was that she and all her family lived quite close to one another. They met regularly if not daily. I was fortunate to have that daily contact with her. That proximity is not a feature of many families today. I am aware of the circumstances that cause this separation. Separation does not diminish in any way the love and affection for one another but a lot of the tales of yesteryear and the wisdom that often goes with it are perhaps lost. A main objective of writing the story of life in my day is to make up for some of that loss. It is very unlikely that my own grandchildren will be familiar with many things that are common knowledge today. It is even more unlikely that they will have any knowledge of life in the periods about which I shall be writing. For the benefit of those youngsters in my family of the future, I may go into detail on some matters to explain to them in greater depth than perhaps seems necessary. There will also be a strong background of family matters.

It was not my original aim that the book should be published. Now that it is, I must apologise to readers who might find it irritating that I dwell in depth on matters that they might consider to be common knowledge. I have not written this book because I did anything of great note but I do hope that the period of my life from 1920 to date [2000] may be of some interest to others in the years to come.

This is an autobiography in three Parts: -

Part 1 - 1920 to 1939.

Part 2 - 1939 to the end of the Second World War in 1945

Part 3 - 1945 to date

My intention was to start the story at the obvious place, the beginning. Yet I delayed so long in starting that I began to wonder whether I would ever reach Part 2, the part that is perhaps the most interesting. I was born a few months after the end of the First World War, fought in the Second World War and I am now into the next Millennium. Though I hope to be around for at least a wee while, I finally decided to begin with Part 2 and to write it as a separate book. Thus here is the account of my war years, from being called up at the beginning of the War, until I was demobbed in 1945. (I shall try to write Parts 1 and 3 before I am called to a higher – or lower – place).

Of course, during the war keeping a diary was forbidden and it is quite likely that I shall not be historically accurate in dates and in the chronological order of events. As regards names, I was not much better at remembering then than I am now but I have done my best, and I have used few specific names, so as to avoid giving offence to anyone still alive.

This book then is simply the story of a civilian called up for military service in World War II; of an ordinary serviceman and his experiences, experiences similar to those of thousands of other servicemen. It is not a history diligently researched in libraries and history books. It is told as it happened and from the viewpoint of an ordinary Marine. It tries to express the feelings and emotions of someone who, very often, had no idea of what was going on all around him, especially in battle, as many of us never did. Indeed, although I was involved in the Battle of Crete, I had no idea what was happening in other parts of Crete until long after the battle. Despite the title, there was nothing heroic in it.

For my family

In dedicating this book to the children of my family of the future, I have a vision of a scene in the Millennium. A wee bairn is curled up in an armchair, engrossed in this story about the experiences of one of his own family in a war away back in distant history. If he were smiling at one of my stories then I would be smiling too. That thought gives me great pleasure and every moment spent in the writing of this book will have been well worth the effort.

Part 1

War is Declared

Chapter 1

The First Year

"…….. this country is now at war with Germany"

Those few words irrevocably changed my life, the life of my parents and of millions of people throughout the world in 1939. The words, uttered by Neville Chamberlain, the Prime Minister, on the 3rd day of September 1939, will be forever etched in my memory. Some people still say that the assassination of John F. Kennedy, President of the United States of America, had such an impact on them that they can still recall where they were when they heard the news. I am sure that for many of my age, the announcement by Chamberlain that war had been declared had the greatest impact of any event in their lives.

I can remember standing in the kitchen of my home in Dalcross Street, Partick, Glasgow. My Mother and Father and I stood silent. The impact was not one of shock. The possibility, or even the probability, of war had hovered over us all since Mr. Chamberlain returned from his peace-seeking visit to Adolf Hitler at Berchtesgarten. As he stood on the steps of the plane on his return, he waved a piece of paper and uttered the famous words "Peace in our time". Many doubted that Hitler, who had ignored international protestations when he invaded Czechoslovakia, would pay attention to British protests when he invaded Poland. Some of my colleagues in the Post Office had already been called up to Militia. A year before 1939, the possibility of war was so great that a Militia force was created. Young men who reached the age of twenty were eligible. Many prayed around this time that the horror of another war might be averted.

These prayers were not answered. So it wasn't the shock of the announcement that stunned us. The three of us, representing two generations, stood stock-still, gazing at that wireless as though we could wish it all away. Not a word was spoken but the reality was slowly beginning to sink in. The future of a normal life as we knew it was gone, never to return. I looked across at my Mum and Dad and saw the expression on their faces. I suddenly realised that they had been through all this before, for them it was the second time around.

Dad had been in the Great War of 1914, the so-called "War to end Wars". Millions of lives were lost in that War and many more were maimed for life. What thoughts must have been going through my parent's minds at that moment? Had all the sacrifices in that horror been in vain? The War to end wars! Yet only twenty years, a blink in eternity, had passed since it ended. Who would have dreamed they would so soon to have to go through it all again?

With the advent of aeroplanes, bringing such tremendous potential for mass destruction, the horror of this war would be worse than ever before. My parents' two sons, with all their young lives in front of them, would be called up soon. They showed no outward sign of emotion, not a word was said and I felt that their thoughts were in unison. How to describe that expression? Sad? Haunting? Bewildered? Disgusted? They would certainly be frightened, at least for their family. No words could adequately describe their emotions.

The silence seemed to last forever. I'll always remember the quiet and poignant scene in that wee kitchen in a Glasgow tenement. If I were able to paint that scene today, fifty-nine years later, I could recall every detail. They stood there so silently, eyes glued to that sightless and wireless instrument of bad news, as though Chamberlain's voice might re-emerge to say that it was all a horrible mistake. It was no mistake. In this war they would both be civilians. They would not be going to war, but this time war would come to them, a war that would have weapons of a hitherto unbelievable potential for destruction. After the bombing of the civilian population in Poland, everyone expected civilians to be in the front line. The time would come when their hearts would pound at the wailing sound of the sirens, heralding the bombs about to fall.

For me it was a different situation. Back in 1935 I had to leave school at fifteen without any qualifications. Although I had a scholarship which paid my fees and books at Hutcheson's Boys Grammar School, Glasgow, the family was in dire financial straits. A fire destroyed the family business, owned by my Grandfather Clark. The business closed and my Grandad retired. My Dad and his two brothers had to find jobs in the middle of what is still looked upon as the greatest economic depression of all times. The depression was hitting the family hard. Dad was working only three days a week. They could not afford to keep me on at school. My pay as an office boy was five shillings a week, a pittance by today's standards. But that pittance, added to saving of the cost of keeping me on at school, kept the family's head above water.

My lack of qualifications made it difficult to find a quality job. But I managed to enter the Civil Service through the Post Office and when the war broke out, I was a Sorting Clerk in Glasgow. This was about the lowest level in the Civil Service and one could only advance by passing entrance examinations to a higher grade. My aim was to pass for entry at the Executive Officer grade.

I studied for a number of years. It was tough going. I was working shifts so I was able to fit in daytime studies at a commercial college. Although it drastically reduced my leisure activities I was strongly motivated because an Executive Officer position in those days was very highly valued. The examination was to take place in September 1939. You may have guessed what transpired next. When war was declared, all Civil Service examinations were cancelled for the duration of the war! Thus all that effort was to no avail – the first of my 'Almosts'.

As I write now, a few months into the year 2000 of the third millennium, I realise how difficult it must be for today's young man of nineteen to understand the intellectual and spiritual turmoil of a nineteen year old potential conscript in 1939. In my case, I was brought up in the Christian faith and had a belief in God who laid down the Commandment: "Thou shalt not kill." Suddenly, seemingly in the space of seconds, we were launching warships with the blessing of the Church on all who sailed in them.

I mention this little saga because it will help you to understand how the lives of young men like me were devastated when war broke out. Suddenly there was no direction, no objectives, no ambition, no motivation. It was difficult to envisage life ahead. There was no need to make plans. Whether you would like to join the Forces was irrelevant. You would be conscripted at the age of 20, unless you declared yourself a conscientious objector. That didn't cross my mind. You couldn't choose which arm of the services you joined; a preference? - yes, a choice? - no.

You might be killed, captured or maimed for life. Gradually the implications of going to war began to dominate one's life. Admittedly there would be a new life in the Forces, but this was war and by no stretch of imagination could it be looked on as any substitute for a career. It was a task that had to be done, hopefully, we thought, only a short and temporary task.

When the outbreak of war was announced, we all expected massive bombing raids. Most people expected that the Germans would mount an immediate bombing campaign, followed by an invasion of the south coast of England. When the sirens sounded their loud wail, warning of enemy aircraft approaching, people dived for air raid shelters. Yet the massive bombing and attempted invasion did not materialise until later and we referred to this period as the "phoney" war.

For young men awaiting a call-up to the services, there was a tremendous change in attitude to life and work. Because the war and matters related to it dominated everything, hopes and ambitions for the future - so important only weeks before - now had no relevance. We tended to live for the day, dancing, playing sports, maybe drinking a bit more than we should or, for some, maybe drinking for the first time. I have to admit that I was quite enjoying all the social activity. Strangely enough, although I was relishing the freedom to pass the time enjoying myself until I was called up to the Forces, I could not concentrate on anything. You missed the lads who were already in the Forces and felt guilty, as though you too should be away.

I disliked the word 'conscription'. It sounded too much like the Navy in the old days when Press Gangs roamed the country recruiting men (willing or not) to man the warships. It was the feeling of wasting our time that prompted Bob Ure, my friend and colleague in the Post Office, to try to volunteer for the Royal Navy even though we would be called up in April. My Dad, being in the Navy in the Great War, might have influenced me to apply for the Navy but I don't think so, because his story of joining the Navy was humorous, yet scarcely inspiring.

He told me that there was a famous poster inviting men to "Join the Navy and see the world". Probably it was a poster left over from peacetime with visions of exotic places in the sunshine. I can't believe that Dad fell for that line in wartime, but he said to himself: "It's as good a reason as any." After his training in Plymouth he saw his name on the notice board. Where would his posting take him? Barbados or Hawaii? The destination was a wee bit nearer home. It was the Scapa Flow, the base of the Grand Fleet in Orkney. Dad thought: "Well, it might be a Battle Cruiser or at least a ship of reasonable size with less chance of a landlubber getting seasick." His luck was still out. A fishing boat converted to a minesweeper became his home for the rest of the war.

The Pentland Firth has a reputation for being one of the stormiest stretches of water in the world. I thought of Dad, out sweeping for mines in a converted fishing boat in the freezing conditions of winter. His war-time experiences may not have been as glamorous as being on a battleship, but I realised that his sojourn at Scapa Flow had been no sinecure. I wonder what he thought the next time he came across that poster with its tempting invitation to see the world.

Bob Ure and I eventually surrendered to our restless and compulsive feelings and trundled along to the Royal Navy recruiting office to volunteer. We were not alone in giving in to those feelings. The Navy was chock-a-block with young lads deciding to volunteer rather than wait for conscription. Because of the great number wanting to join the Navy, we were told that anyone approaching the age of 20 should go home and wait for their call up papers. It was unlikely that we would be "called up" to the Navy, so it was suggested that we might consider joining the Marines. Ignorance is bliss. We both thought that it would be much the same as being in the Navy. It seemed far better to be sailing about in ships than slogging it in the infantry. How naïve could one be?

The invasion of Norway by the Germans caused my parents a lot of anxiety. The war was coming closer. Just before my birthday, reports of a landing in Namos in Norway by the Royal Marines hit the headlines. The fact that it was a Royal Marines expedition increased their anxiety about what the future might have in store for me. I confess to having thoughts along the same lines, but already I was already adopting the philosophic attitude of those on the Western Front during the Great War. When bombing or gunfire was very fierce, a fatalistic approach was: "If a bomb has my name on it, there is nothing I can do, so there is no use in worrying….. "

During the period of the "phoney" war, many held hopes that the Germans would be halted by the much-publicised Maginot Line and that an invasion of Britain would thus be prevented. This false sense of security was soon dissipated when the Germans by-passed the Maginot Line and made a successful and rapid attack through the Low Countries. The Allied forces were pushed back to the shores of France, and France surrendered. The British could not hold back the Germans single-handed and so the evacuation of British troops took place at Dunkirk about the end of May 1940.

The Royal Navy, assisted by a flotilla of small civilian ships, successfully managed to evacuate many soldiers who might otherwise have spent the rest of the war in a prisoner of war camp. Thousands of servicemen were not so lucky and did land up in POW camps. Although the evacuation was rightly hailed as a magnificent achievement in military terms, the defeat was a disaster. It changed the whole atmosphere in Britain. After Dunkirk many people felt very despondent. The possibility of an invasion preceded by heavy bombing now became the threat uppermost in everyone's mind.

Chapter 2

The Royal Marines

Chatham

April duly arrived and my call up papers dropped through the letterbox. I can't remember the exact date but it was after Dunkirk. As soon as I entered the house I knew by the look on my Mum's face that they had come. Bob Ure and I received orders to report on the same day to the Royal Marine barracks at Chatham. The occupation of the Low Countries and France had dramatically changed the whole situation and the families in our wee street were very worried when any of the lads left to join the Forces.

It was a big event and all the neighbours were either in the street or at the windows. It was goodbye to Civvy Street (civilian life) and a sad farewell to family and friends. I had a big lump in my throat. I must admit, however, that when Bob and I boarded the London train, the completely new experience excited us. I don't recall much of the actual departure in the train but I do recall arriving at the gates of the Royal Marines. The guard was a huge man. He had a peaked cap and wore it in the typical manner of the Royal Marines and the Guards. The peak was worn so far down over the forehead that, to see anyone properly, you had to lift your head. I assume that it was to meet the constant command - "Head up and shoulders back". There was no doubt that wearing the peaked cap so far down kept the head up. The guard, looking down his nose at me from a great height, certainly made me feel that I had just crawled out of the woodwork. Royal Marines, here I come.

The training that lay ahead did not particularly bother me. That was mainly because I very much underestimated the degree of fitness expected and the discipline considered necessary to change a raw recruit into a fighting machine up to the Royal Marines' standard. I had always kept myself fit and the outdoor life taught me how to look after myself, at least as far as cooking etc. As a Staff Sergeant in the Boy's Brigade, drilling had been a big part of the training. I had passed exams on the subject but I wasn't daft enough to let any of these thoughts slip out. I had no illusions about the reaction of a Royal Marine Sergeant if you gave him even a suspicion that you thought the Marine training was a piece of cake. The wisdom of my silence was soon to become apparent.

A Corporal took us in hand. Our first task was to be fitted out with our uniforms and to collect our boots and a hundred and one items of equipment. I was amazed at the amount of gear and I wondered how on earth all that lot could be fitted into a pack. I was soon to learn that not only could the lot be fitted into the pack but also that every item would come out as neatly as it went in. The new and very raw looking recruits gathered in a barrack room awaiting their fate. What an assembly we were, the long and the short and the tall. A real cross-section of the conscript population.

The variety of clothes was as great as the differences in physical appearance. Once the civvy clothes disappeared and we stood together in uniform, it was amazing the immediate difference it made. From then on the word uniform applied not just to our clothes, even our personalities were submerged. We now belonged to the same outfit. It was a bit like going to school for the first time, except that the word "Why" (always encouraged at school) now brought a slightly different response from the NCO's.

When the Platoon Sergeant walked into the barrack room, he immediately imposed his personality on us. There was no doubt who was in charge and what his reaction would be if we did not come up to his expectations. For the next nine weeks it would be his responsibility to turn this motley crew into Marines. I had no illusions that we would curse him as he drove us to a level of fitness and hardness we had never dreamed possible. Any cursing would have to be under our breath but there was no doubt about our being cursed.

For the next nine weeks we would be confined to barracks, nine weeks of hard, unstinting slog without shore leave (even when ashore, the Marines referred to leave as if you were aboard ship). Then, and only then, would those judged fit to represent the Royal Marines be allowed to march out of the barracks as individuals.

The process of grinding us into shape began at once. All were ordered to get a 'haircut' - immediately. That was a euphemistic term, because your hair was not cut it was shorn. Looking in the mirror I realised that I would now have to drop the Mr. Clark and become 'Clark, CHX 100651'. As though tattooed on my brain, that number sticks with me until this day.

Normal noise levels ceased to exist. Commands were shouted at a pitch deliberately calculated to make you jump out of your skin. Some people called the training a brutalising process. Our Sergeant was tough, very tough, but I found him fair. Others were not so fair and their undisputed power could be misused. If you performed badly or slacked, they could make you want to dig a big hole and vanish, whereas our Sergeant praised you if you did well or tried your best. I was quite prepared for the necessity to jump to attention immediately a command was given. In a battle situation it could mean the difference between life and death. Something I was to appreciate later in the war. What I was not prepared for was the way that they drove home that requirement - by highlighting the need always to accept without question even the smallest of details.

I could never lose my instinct to ask questions about why I was asked to do anything. I understood the purpose behind their methods and I tried to react accordingly. In the back of my mind I wondered how I would react to a command that I felt was morally wrong. Fortunately that problem never arose during my spell in the Services although several times during my spell in prison camp in Germany it caused me anxiety.

In turning the rabble into a Rookie Squad fit to enter 'the Holy

Area', the sergeant had a deadline to meet. Eventually he met it, and a very nervous Rookie Squad had to fall in for the first time on the huge parade ground. All the other Squads looked so smart, so confident and to us they seemed as though they had been drilling for a lifetime. The senior squad, known as the Passing Out Squad, moved as one man and was a real showpiece. I looked at our Sergeant and thought what an impossible task lay ahead of him, transforming us into a squad that looked something like the Senior Squad. He seemed impassive, showing no signs of concern. Probably he had lost count of the rookie squads he had turned out. For a good number of us the most terrifying prospect of all was about to commence - drilling on that massive parade ground.

A raw recruit had difficulty in accepting a culture and discipline foreign to him. In peacetime recruits volunteered for service. They had chosen the Service as their life and career and had to accept its demands if they wanted to make any advancement. By contrast, recruits in wartime were conscripted. Most, like myself, had a different motivation. In any case, it was pointless to try to buck the system, it only made things worse. I also hoped that I would survive this war, that it would be short, and that I would soon return to civilian life. Had I possessed second sight I would have thought differently.

That early summer of 1940 was warm, sunny and bright. Much of our training took place on the open areas around Chatham. I was very fit before I joined up but I was fit for sport and leisure activities such as football and touring the country by bicycle. I came to take on a different view of fitness as our training advanced. The weather may have been marvellous for the tourist but it made us sweat. One occasion when we even sweated in anticipation was when the order of the day was "Full Marching Order", which meant we had to carry the maximum amount of kit in our packs. As the march still had to be completed in the usual time a high average speed was needed and that was no mean feat, a feat that frequently ended up with blistered feet!

Because we were confined to barracks until we had reached a certain level of efficiency, our existence was somewhat monastic. We were very preoccupied in just trying to keep up with the arduous and demanding training regimen. The world outside was, albeit temporarily, not our concern. If we needed any reminder of the end purpose of our training, it hung daily over our heads.

A lot of our training took place on the Chatham Downs. Above us the Battle of Britain was being enacted. It was a most encouraging and morale-boosting sight. Herr Goering had been boasting for years about the might and superiority of his air armada. Events up until now seemed to support his boasts. The Royal Air Force was outnumbered as the German planes came across the English Channel every day in waves. At first we were made to dive for cover as cannon shells, bullets and burning planes came cascading down out of the sky. Later we just carried on and only stopped when it looked a bit too close for comfort.

During our breaks we lay back and watched the spectacle as though it was a film. The Spitfires were like terriers. Although it was a great encouragement to witness this historic battle, we were saddened by the British losses, as fighter after fighter came screaming down. Only later did we realise the extent of the sacrifice of young lives being made in the sky above us.

Our Squad was approaching the final stages of the training course. We had successfully undertaken a very long march despite many blistered feet and aching limbs. We had become inured to these conditions. Now we were not only fit but also hardened.

Praise was never given nor expected. You knew that the Sergeant was pleased, not so much by what he said as by what he did not say. At last we were considered fit to be allowed out into the big wide world on our own. We were given shore leave. We proudly marched down into Chatham to look for the nearest pub.

I had a bit of a problem. Because I had always been committed to sport, I was not keen on alcohol or smoking although I had learned to take the odd drink, just enough to avoid being socially ostracised by my friends. A non-smoking and non-drinking Marine was not a particularly popular bloke and I sank further in the popularity stakes when I decided not to take the traditional tot of rum. When you entered the navy or the Marines, the option was given of either taking the traditional Navy tot of rum or taking three pence per day in lieu. I had no hesitation in plumping for the cash. That was the wrong choice as far as the rum drinkers were concerned. Nobody told me what was expected of non-drinkers. I did not know that non-drinkers took their tot and, if they didn't want it, they passed it on. My tastes in these respects meant that I became very unpopular. In a close-knit community the pressure to conform is very strong.

Just as we were coming to the end of our training, Bob and I were told to report to the Office. A summons usually spelt trouble. You marched into the Office in trepidation. A Marine was pleased if the only thing known about him was his name in the records. It was unheard of to be called to the Office during recruit training unless you had committed some dastardly offence. Bob and I were more than a little curious. We were even more taken aback when the reason was revealed.

A new outfit called the Mobile Naval Base Defence Organisation, (the MNBDO), had been formed and we were being posted to Portsmouth Depot immediately to join it.

We learned later that the MNBDO was to be a completely self-supporting unit containing elements of the Fleet, Marine infantry and the Royal Marine Ack-Ack (anti-aircraft guns) and searchlights. It was the brainchild of Winston Churchill.

The German Army, under General Rommel, was advancing rapidly in Libya, the Allied Army was retreating equally rapidly and Tobruck was in danger of falling. It was intended that the MNBDO would move in from seaward to prevent it falling into German hands. All that we knew at the time was that the MNBDO had an Anti-Aircraft unit of Bofors guns who would have attached to them new equipment that could greatly improve their ability to beam in on their target. It was called a Radio Direction Finder.

We were baffled as to why we should be chosen. It turned out that our job in the Post Office was "Sorting Clerk and Telegraphist". It was no use telling the Officer that, although Telegraphist was in our title, we were actually only Sorting Clerks, sorting letters and parcels. He had obviously made up his mind, so Radio Direction Finder operators we became.

I was disappointed that the posting to Portsmouth was considered so urgent that we were not allowed to finish the last part of our training course. Although we were seldom parted from our rifles, we hadn't had much training with live ammunition. I can only recall firing five rounds. Probably "Training completed" was entered on our record and Chatham would feel satisfied that its part of the job was done. My expectations remained unfulfilled. I had wanted so much to have as much experience as possible before I met up with the battle trained Wehrmacht, another of my 'Almosts'.

Portsmouth

When we reported to the Marine barracks at Portsmouth, there was no RDF equipment available so we could not commence training. I was very disappointed about the lack of communication between Portsmouth and Chatham concerning the equipment. We could have done the complete training course, perhaps an unusual complaint from a Marine.

I had no doubt that the Marines' methods produced an efficient and physically fit person. The Marines looked for more than ordinary fitness. They looked for that hardness to push you to what you thought was your limit and then they pushed you a bit more. I wanted to be hard. I wanted to learn all that there was to know about handling firearms. I wanted to give myself every chance to survive.

When war was declared, I had a mental picture that one day I might well be in the situation of a Wild West movie: "High Noon", kill or be killed. Until I joined the Marines I had never had a gun in my hand. Now my only motivation in training was to be prepared for the day when I might be in that situation. Given the goal that I set myself, it was galling to finish my training with only a short acquaintance of the firing range. The one piece of advice that stuck in my mind was to hold your breath, keep the gun tight into your shoulder and squeeze that trigger as though it was a feather. I had fired a measly few rounds from a 1914 Lee Enfield rifle. Would I some day face a skilled marksman when, as in the OK Corral shoot out, only the winner walks away? Hopefully I would gain more experience but I put these thoughts aside and concentrated on the new task that lay ahead of me.

Released from the intensity of Chatham and with no training meantime at Portsmouth, this was a short but very relaxed period. With the Germans in occupation across the Channel, there was periodic bombing. The prospect of the German invasion and the heavy bombing that would precede it caused considerable anxiety. One false alarm in one of the main streets was amusing. The sound of sirens in the immediate locality caused people to make a beeline for the air raid shelters and illustrated how nervous people had become. The rush slowed down when it was realised that the sound of the sirens was coming through an open door in a cinema in which a Newsreel film was being shown.

It was interesting to walk along the seafront at Southsea, look across the English Channel and wonder whether the German hordes were amassing for an invasion. I suppose we were a part of history just like the people centuries ago who stood on this coast looking across the Channel, speculating on whether the Spanish Armada was entering the Channel. They couldn't have been any more nervous than the people of Portsmouth were in 1940.

The new task facing Bob and me was the main subject of our conversation. We decided that the Radio Direction Finder might be an interesting subject. It was the forerunner of Radar. The disappointment of our abrupt departure from Chatham gradually lessened. Another interesting encounter happened when we were walking along the sea front. A little man who seemed very familiar passed us. Our attention was drawn to him because he had an entourage and we assumed that he must be very important. It turned out that he was the Emperor of Ethiopia. When Italy invaded his country, he had to evacuate in a hurry. I believe he stayed in Britain until the end of the war.

Our period of relaxation soon ended. Apparently there was no experience of RDF in the Marines so we were posted for training in RDF to an Anti Aircraft Unit near Nottingham. It wasn't too sophisticated, at least compared to Radar. During our training the Germans carried out a massive air attack on Coventry. Obviously trainees were not allowed to operate the equipment during the raid but it was a useful experience to watch the action.

We hadn't got very far with our training when we were called back to Portsmouth. Preparations were on hand to embark the MNBDO as soon as possible. We gathered that the situation in Libya must have been deteriorating. Once again I had not finished a course and I was beginning to feel really frustrated. I had hoped that there would be opportunities to gain more experience on the long sea journey and certainly before we moved into the Middle East Sector. At present I was strong on theory but weak in practice. The incomplete course on RDF was yet another of my "Almosts".

Chapter 3

The Atlantic Convoy

The River Clyde

When we arrived back in Portsmouth there was great activity. Rumours abounded. Bob and I had indirect confirmation that we were headed for foreign climes. We were told that a convoy would be leaving from Glasgow and because we were Glaswegians we were sent on the advance guard so that we could pay a brief visit to our families. Our ship was the SS Bergensfjord.

The heavy air raids made travelling by train a hazardous business. The train was absolutely packed, with far more passengers than seats. Many of the passengers were women so most of the servicemen had to stand in the corridors. I can recall that the train was so full for the first half of the journey that I sometimes stood for long periods on one foot. I can't remember how long it took but it was a very tired and sore Marine who finally arrived at his home in Partick, Glasgow. What a welcome when I turned up without warning. What joy it was to be home again, even though it was going to be a very brief visit. It was a quick hello and goodbye - for God knows how many years

Many convoys were mustered on the Clyde. Security was very tight in the Glasgow docks. Because of the prevalence of German cruisers and U-boats in the Atlantic, Glasgow became a haven for German spies. There were many eyes and ears anxious to pass information to the enemy. How easily that information could leak was obvious when I told my folks that I was on embarkation leave.

My Mum and Dad were delighted to see me. My comment on the tight security made them laugh. Dad said that, although Glaswegians were very careful about spreading information, they were aware of impending convoy movements. For example Dad knew that a huge convoy was gathering in the Firth of Clyde. The Shieldhall Docks, where the Bergensfjord was berthed, was opposite the famous Singer Sewing Machine factory in Clydebank where Dad worked. Many ships berthed upstream before they headed down the Clyde to join convoys gathering in the estuary.

He often watched ships being commissioned and servicemen gathering. Glad as they were to see me even for the short time, they were also both sad and worried. They knew full well that my short stay and the large convoy gathering in the Clyde could only mean that I was on that convoy.

When I said my farewells, I could not tell them where I was going. But they knew that if I was on a convoy I would be going far away and probably for a long time. For the first time since I joined up, I was really choked as I walked out of Dalcross Street with family and even the neighbours waving goodbye and openly crying.

Goodbye to Blighty

I had a pleasant surprise before we left the Clyde. The huge clock on the tower of the Singer Sewing Machine factory was well known. My Dad told me long ago that the figure six on the clock acted as a large door used for maintenance work. He said that if he saw the convoy moving during the day, he would make an attempt to be at the door and give me a wave. I was on the lookout for Dad but the really unexpected surprise was hearing from my Mum.

A call went up from the guard on the gangway of the ship. "Marine Alex Clark from Glasgow report to the gangway?" I was very puzzled. What on earth prompted that call? He handed me a parcel and said: "Your old mum left this at the dock gates. She says it's your favourite cake, you lucky bastard." I had a feeling it would be a very long time before I tasted her cakes again.

Perhaps that final farewell gesture of a gift of food was her way of saying that although I was a man going off to war, to her I would always be the bairn she mothered all these lean years. She had an awfully persuasive tongue and she must have melted the heart of the security guard at the gate to make him accept the parcel. To cap that lovely motherly thought, when the Bergensfjord was passing the Singer Factory I looked up to the clock. I could not see the figure Six. The door must be open and I thought that I saw three little dots. I assumed that Dad was there. I was indeed a lucky lad to have such caring parents. I was fair choked. The memory of that visit and the chance to say goodbye before my departure was a great comfort to me in later very stressful times.

The SS Bergensfjord sailed past Greenock and the Dumbarton Rock, a Rock that down the centuries of Scottish history had seen warships coming up and down the Clyde. My thoughts as we entered the Clyde Estuary were not on history. I recalled many happier days as a wee boy, sailing "Doon the Watter" aboard paddle steamers with romantic names from Sir Walter Scott's novels, the Jeannie Deans, the Waverley or the first non-paddle steamer, the Duchess of Montrose. Our destination then was no further than the holiday resorts of the Clyde estuary, Largs, Rothesay, the Kyles of Bute and the Isle of Arran. What lovely days those were.

As the convoy gathered in the estuary I had time to let the beautiful scenery soak into my memory. Looking across to the Cowal peninsula with its background of magnificent mountains, the memories of boyhood cycling adventures to the newly formed Youth Hostels came flooding back.

Although I felt sad and nostalgic to be sailing away from the beautiful Clyde estuary, I was grateful that I was given the chance to see it again before I left home. I was really very lucky, lucky to have had a last opportunity to see the beautiful land where I was born, lucky to have been able to say a final goodbye to my parents, lucky to have had that last gesture by my Mum. Although I was going off to the wars, she still felt that I was her wee laddie who needed something like his favourite cake to cheer him up.

The ship sailed out into the Atlantic and the Bergensfjord rose to the ocean swell. The ship was packed with troops and we were squeezed into every corner. We had not ventured very far from the West Coast of Ireland when a light storm blew up. The increased swell created havoc among those who were subject to seasickness. The numbers seriously affected surprised me. The Norwegian Skipper was sympathetic to all those who were seasick and felt that it was an insult to their manhood. He let it be known that, although he had been going to sea since he was a boy, he was always seasick whenever he left harbour. Nice chap to be concerned, even if it was not true.

On one occasion when we were in mid Atlantic, a storm warning was announced. I had often read the description, mountainous seas. I interpreted that as a description meaning very large waves. Under the blackening sky, the wind, increasing to gale force, drove the waves with ever-greater intensity. The bow of the Bergensfjord, a 15,000 ton ship, rode higher and higher up the huge waves and came down with a thump, sending spray over the ship. Hardly mountainous waves, I thought disparagingly.

The Bergensfjord was quite a large ship but as the storm worsened and the waves got larger, she rose up the waves until her bow was clean out of the water and she seemed to hang in suspension for ages. As the wave passed under her she suddenly crashed down with an almighty bang. A shudder ran through her as though she would split in two. The noise of the wind rose to a crescendo.

For the crew on duty up on deck it was probably nothing to write home about. But the only time that I had been in a boat in rough water was in a wee rowing boat "Doon the Watter" in a high wind off Largs pier. No way did it prepare me for this. Now the description "mountainous" seemed absolutely accurate. It was terrifying.

Below decks only the brave or the foolhardy stayed in the wildly swaying hammocks and that was not for long. The place stank with the smell of seasickness. A fair number, who had previously been cock-a-hoop because they had not so far been affected by the ocean swell, succumbed to the storm conditions and were in a bad way. This included a few of the new part-time Marines. None of them was singing the Royal Marines tune: "A life on the ocean wave, a home on the rolling deep", at least not with any marked enthusiasm. That experience and the whole voyage brought home to me vividly the very special courage and bravery of merchant seamen

The convoy was made up of a variety of ships because the losses suffered by the Merchant Fleet due to submarine attacks were very high. Many ships were brought out of retirement. Most of these were safe but speed was not one of their strong points. On a convoy as large as ours, the naval escort had a real problem because the convoy could only proceed at the speed of the slowest ship. We used to enjoy the Naval escorts wheeling at high speed, rounding up the stragglers like a sheep dog working the sheep into a pen. A slow convoy could be a sitting duck for a submarine.

By now the convoy should have been heading South but for some time it was still heading West. The escorts were chasing stragglers even more assiduously than usual and signals were flashing angrily. A rumour spread that a German cruiser was in the area.

We now saw at first hand how difficult it was for the few naval escorts to keep the convoy in order and how extremely vulnerable merchant ships were to submarine attack and surface raiders. Most ships had only one pitifully small gun positioned in the stern of the boat. If the naval escorts did not pick up a sub on their radar, the first indication of its presence was often when a torpedo hit a merchantman or troop ship. In that situation the troops were justified in being apprehensive particularly because they were always confined below decks during red alerts, not the best place to be when torpedoes paid an uninvited call. Even the crews, who might have been through this many times and were hardened to the ever-imminent dangers, were understandably touchy and were subconsciously waiting for the strike of that silent and unseen enemy, the submarine.

The convoy should by now have been heading down past the Med

(Mediterranean) to our first port of call, Freetown in East Africa. The news that a German battle cruiser might be in the vicinity meant that we were diverted West until we were near Nova Scotia. With so many troops on board, the increased distance meant that food and water supplies were very low. Fortunately there was no more word of enemy activity and the convoy turned and slowly headed east again. We gave a combined hail and farewell wave to Nova Scotia from Auld Scotia, heading hopefully for a landfall at Freetown and a welcome halt to replenish our supplies.

Freetown

As the convoy steamed east and south the temperature rose each day. We sweltered in the blistering heat and the reduced water rations made life a bit difficult. Long before we reached Freetown we sensed that distinctive and powerful smell of Africa.

Eventually we sailed into Freetown harbour where the convoy had to be restocked and refuelled. Shore leave was out of the question but it was a pleasant respite from life on the open sea. We hadn't yet acquired a sailor's rolling walk but it was a change to be in still waters. For many of us who had not been outside Scotland it was very interesting to observe life in a tropical African port. The natives rushed out in boats to sell us fresh fruit. That was welcome. Another attraction was the native boys who loved to dive down into the clear blue sea to retrieve coins.

An embarrassment for some of the Marines, myself included, was caused by an Officer who had the bright idea that it would be a diversion for Marines who had not been to sea to be taught how to handle a longboat. He soon wished that he had never dreamed up the idea. Hundreds of soldiers lined the rails of the convoy ships obviously thinking that a race was being arranged to give the Marines an opportunity to demonstrate their prowess at handling the boats. The experienced Marines licked their lips in gleeful anticipation of the fun and frolics about to happen. The inexperienced Marines in the boats caught crabs and got into all sorts of a pickle. Chaos broke out and in no time the boats were going round in circles. The image of the Marines took a severe dent.

An amazing coincidence in connection with this incident happened to me recently. I was sitting in the local Golf Club clubhouse in Ballater, situated in the foothills of the Grampian Mountains. At a nearby table my good friend, Norman Thain, was reciting a story about having sailed in a convoy from Glasgow in 1941. I couldn't believe my ears. Surely it would be too much of a coincidence that we were both in the same convoy all these years ago? I tapped Norman on the shoulder.

"When you were in Freetown, Norman, do you recall seeing Royal Marines in longboats going round in circles?"

"I did that," says Norman. "I laughed my head off, the Royal Marines of all folk. Don't tell me you were there."

"I certainly was there." I said. "I was one of the unfortunate beginners in a longboat, unintentionally providing first class entertainment to hundreds of appreciative but unsympathetic bystanders".

Amazing how often these cross-roads occur in your life. Two people who had been friends for more than twenty years only now finding out that they had shared a unique experience in wartime over half a century ago. However, we have made up for lost time and established a very good friendship, despite losing so many bets to one another on the golf course. I regret that I have now lost my good friend, Norman. He passed away recently.

South Africa

The convoy set sail, the troops replenished bodily and mentally. Our next port of call was Cape Town, then on to Durban and round the Cape of Good Hope on the way to Egypt. It was still a long journey but already the men were thinking about what lay ahead. It could hardly be called a luxury tour but it was free and very interesting.

We were enjoying the uninterrupted sunshine that warmed the hearts of a Scot who often saw snow in May. I was anticipating the pleasant prospect of seeing, however briefly, two of South Africa's main ports, Cape Town and Durban. The well-travelled older Marines told us that a visit to these ports was something to write home about.

For the present we wiped out all thoughts of the unpleasantness that might soon be our lot and just lived for the moment. Adopting that approach, along with a sense of humour, was probably a major factor in the survival of many men, both during the voyage and later. The voyage was uneventful and as pleasant as you would expect life on a packed troopship to be. Indeed my main memory of that part of our journey was the "Crossing the Equator" ceremony.

The excitement aboard the Bergensfjord mounted as we finally approached Cape Town. After a voyage that seemed to have lasted an aeon, we were soon about to walk again on "Terra Firma".

A wonderful sight greeted us as we entered Cape Town harbour. The sun shone out of a clear blue sky on green hills alive with a riot of colour from tropical flowers and vegetation and on the white houses, set against the vivid marine blue/green of a sparkling sea. The flat top of the Table Mountain made a lovely backdrop to a landfall after so long at sea, appreciated all the more because we were not aware that the inhabitants gave their hearts to the troops passing through on their long and dangerous journey to the war in the African Desert.

We were given leave to go ashore and as we passed out of the dockyard gates a crowd awaited us. We were delighted with their friendly and hospitable treatment.

As we sailed out of the harbour at the end of a very pleasant visit, the green backcloth of the Table Mountain behind Capetown presented a colourful picture in the bright sunshine. We were most grateful for the encouragement given to young lads going to war.

The convoy moved westward for the journey round the Cape of

Good Hope and on to Durban. The severity of gales around the Cape have earned it a frightening reputation. I had often read about the terrible conditions endured by the sailing ships of olden days rounding the Cape.

In our ignorance we thought that we had been blooded in the severe storms of the Atlantic. I was sure that there would be no problems for us on a modern ship the size of the Bergensfjord. My cocksure attitude was about to be shattered. As we sailed out of Cape Town a beautiful sunny day and a calm sea lulled us into a false sense of security. Just as in the North Atlantic storms, the wind rose as a gale approached and suddenly the sky on the horizon blackened, as the wind intensity developed the waves grew larger and larger.

Those who had rounded the Cape before knew what was in store. As the winds reached gale force, huge waves lashed the ship making it bob about like a cork. Many more of us were affected by seasickness this time but I won't repeat the gory details. Although I was not too badly affected, I shall never again hold any disparaging thoughts about seasick landlubbers. Having recovered our equilibrium during the pleasant stay in Cape Town, we were now back to square one.

Once we rounded the Cape the weather calmed and the thoughts of those in command turned to the job awaiting us in Egypt. Practice and training exercises took up more of our time. An announcement was made that a session would be held on dealing with stoppages on the Lewis machine gun, a gun with a great reputation. Although it was another 1914 war relic like our Lee Enfield rifle, I was delighted to have a chance to learn how to handle it, especially after my earlier disappointment that firearms training had been shortened.

My delight was short-lived because it was only a lecture. The Sergeant whipped through the myriad of stoppages in no time flat as though the bugle call: "Come to the cookhouse door, boys" might be sounded at any moment! I can't say that I blamed him. After all, he knew that we were RDF operators and unlikely to be at the front line of any action. For him, the object of the lecture was just to pass the time. For me it was another disappointment and subsequent events made me think that perhaps my desire to be efficient in small arms was due to second sight.

The last port of call before we reached Egypt was Durban, a very different place from Cape Town but the welcome was equally warm. A large crowd awaited us at the dockyard. The locals came forward and invited us to come along to their homes for a meal. Their friendliness and hospitality was marvellous.

When at last the time came for us to leave, the climax of our visit was even more emotional. As we left the harbour the long breakwater was lined with people who came to bid us a fond farewell. A lovely lady, all dressed in white, sang a beautiful song. Apparently she sang for all convoys as they left the harbour. She became famous to thousands of troops as the Lady in White. It was a magnificent scene.

Again the sun was shining and the colourful houses and flowers made a lovely background against the deep blue of the sky. I will never forget the beautiful Lady in White as she stood silhouetted against that sky at the end of the breakwater. As she sang her haunting song her melodious voice came so clear across the water to our ship. All eyes aboard ship were riveted on her and on the crowds on the harbour wall.

The scene faded slowly into the distance. We were all choked up. We did not look at one another as the many tears were brushed away. Hardened soldiers are not supposed to shed tears but most of us were far from hardened. We were hardly out of our teens, now riven from the peaceful environment of a family home and plummeted into a war not of our making.

No doubt there were many young men in the enemy camp just as tearful as they left behind their homes and loved ones. Some memories stand out forever in one's mind and the memory of that scene stayed with me throughout the many dark moments of the next four years.

Just as Vera Lynn became a symbol of home to all allied soldiers in the war, the Lady in White on the Durban breakwater was an inspiration to all the soldiers who were privileged to see and hear her. Even as I write now, I still feel the emotion of that farewell.

I recently saw a film of a ceremonial celebration in Cape Town on the fiftieth anniversary of the war. I believe that a monument or plaque was erected to the memory of that lovely lady, probably on the very spot at the end of the breakwater where she so often stood.

I lingered long on deck to see Durban disappear slowly below the horizon. That short visit made such a great impression on me that I determined, if I should survive this war, that I would seriously consider any opportunity for emigration to South Africa. After the war the opportunity did occur but I missed it and another chance never came my way.

Chapter 4

Egypt

Whither Bound?

With Durban away aft we headed north for the Red Sea and the Suez Canal. The heat at the Equator was hard to bear. The humidity in the Red Sea made it particularly unbearable and I was glad when we eventually disembarked at Port Tauficq in the Suez Canal.

The atmosphere in the MNBDO suddenly changed. We had been at sea for a long time and most of us had never been engaged in action. We had often been in dangerous situations but we were still really spectators, spectators who had supported and cheered on the Royal Navy or, earlier, the RAF during the Battle of Britain. It would not be long now before the purpose of our long journey from Britain would be fulfilled and we would be heavily involved in battle.

By all accounts, there would be no shortage of action in the desert after a short voyage through the Suez Canal, into the Mediterranean and Westwards to Tobruck. This time was one of preparation and there was a strong unsettled feeling, a feeling that we had spent an awful long time getting here and now it was time to get to grips with the job. As far as we knew, the RDF equipment was still aboard ship and that was a pity, because Bob and I could have done with a lot more practice.

One of our leisure activities was football, usually just knock about stuff. Some competition arrived when an Indian regiment stationed nearby, the Maharajah of Bhopal's Regiment, challenged the Marines to a football match. I was chosen to play. The pitch was hard packed sand, almost like concrete. When we lined up I was astounded to see that my opponent had no footwear at all! I wouldn't have called myself a soft hearted player by any means but, when he came near and I saw his bare feet, I couldn't bring myself to tackle the poor bloke with my boots. I held back a bit, but he had no intention of holding back. He clobbered me with his bare feet and I fell to the ground in agony. He had never worn boots in his life until he joined the army. His feet were like iron and I just managed to hold on until the end of the match.

Bob and I went to a local pub to celebrate our 21st birthdays, only a couple of days apart. Not surprisingly it wasn't quite the usual 21st slap up meal with champagne that the occasion merited, actually just a pint of warm beer.

The occasion made it easy for me for once to remember the date of an event. A posting appeared on the notice board. My name was on the notice board but surprisingly Bob's name was not. We never found out why we should be split up since we were both RDF operators and there were few of them. I thought that perhaps my posting was an advance party to Tobruck and Bob would follow on. I was to report in full battle order, ready to embark.

Obviously notices of movements cannot contain details of any sort. Later I was told, to my utter amazement, that our destination was not to be the front at Tobruck. It was the Island of Crete. Why on earth we were going to Crete when we understood that the MNBDO was created specifically for the situation in the desert? That is still a mystery. It was another case of 'Ours not to reason why, ours but to do or die," if I am quoting correctly. So it was goodbye to Bob. I thought that he would follow me to Crete. At one time it looked as if we would go through the whole war together. We did not meet again until after the war.

Part 2

Crete

Chapter 5

The Battle

The Calm before the Storm

Sailing through the Suez Canal was both interesting and instructive. I had considered the River Clyde to be a busy thoroughfare but the volume of traffic on the Suez Canal was tremendous. All sorts of craft sailed up and down the river, pleasure steamers, speed boats, rowing boats, Arab dhows, Egyptian fishing boats, small and large cargo ships, destroyers and many Naval ships, flying the flags of many nations. The noise of their hooters and sirens was only surpassed by the hubbub that floated across the Canal from all the places we passed. "Doon the Watter" to Gourock and Largs, on the Clyde, may have equalled the noise on the Suez but only on the Glasgow Fair Week.

As we approached the exit to the Mediterranean a dolphin joined us. It dived up and down and in and out across the bows of our ship. The dolphin was famous and all the sailors looked for it as they came to the exit from the canal. It accompanied every ship. Sailors have many superstitions. This dolphin was one of them. Sailors would be very unhappy to sail out into the Med if that dolphin did not appear to escort them out. I am not usually superstitious but in my current situation I embraced that one. The dolphin maintained its position until we were well out of the canal and I watched it as we went clear of the canal. It circled the boat and then disappeared, as if to say,: "Mission completed". I was fascinated and quite sorry to see it depart. Maybe my long spell at sea was making me as superstitious as the sailors.

In the Atlantic the presence of submarines was a big concern. In the Mediterranean the German Air Force was dominant, mainly because they were now able to use the airfields in newly occupied Greece. The warning of an approaching plane was sounded. I was below decks at the time but the stern gunner told me how near we were to being sunk. It was a seaplane carrying a torpedo. When the torpedo missed us it was so close that it must have passed right under the stern. Someone up there must have been on our side.

The Island of Crete came into view. A massive mountain range dominated the skyline. I could have been coming home and looking at Sutherland on the West Coast of Scotland, except that there was no mist and the temperature was nearly 30 degrees centigrade. White cumulus clouds capped the mountains and, as they moved over the tops, it seemed as though the mountains were moving. They were very much higher than the Scottish Mountains and not quite so rugged. I stood, spellbound, and thought how I would love to explore them. I came back to the present, remembering where I was and that this was not a Cook's tour. I little realised that I would get to know these mountains intimately, in circumstances far removed from the enjoyment of my mountains back home.

The North of the Island came into view and soon we would be reaching Suda Bay, our destination. We understood that the RAF had some sort of force on the island and I hoped it could give us cover because Suda Bay was well within reach of German planes operating from Greece. Most of us were completely unaware that the situation was so desperate.

As we approached Suda Bay I soon saw evidence of just how desperate the situation was. The first sight was a small sunken ship, probably sunk by the Luftwaffe. Worse was to follow. As we sailed into the bay, we were horrified to see that it was littered with the wrecks of ships of all shapes and sizes. The smoke was still rising from some of them, obviously the result of recent attacks from the air. We were completely devastated by the sight of all these wrecked ships, mostly cargo ships with little or no defences.

The sight that really saddened the Marines was that of the HMS York, sunk and lying half in and half out of the water, like a wee model

Suda Bay. Bombed ships sunk and burning.

Photograph courtesy of the Imperial War Museum

Suda Bay. HMS York sunk.

Photograph courtesy of the Imperial War Museum

sailing boat stuck in the mud of a boating pond. You felt that a battleship like the York should only go down at the hands of another mighty battleship or a massive attack from the air. I heard later that it was not the Luftwaffe that sunk her but the Italians, using small boats loaded with explosives.

The extent of the damage in Suda Bay and the apparent ability of the German air force to strike at will, had a tremendous effect on us, particularly as few of us had yet been blooded in war. The evidence of the overwhelming superiority in numbers of the German Airforce was dramatically and tragically evident.

We were very quiet. While the realisation of what lay ahead of us was beginning to sink in, a big question was on everyone's lips. Where on earth was the RAF? Little did we know how small a force they were. It seems that they had only a very small number of fighters on the island and the emphasis now was on the word "had". They had either been shot down or had left for Egypt. The lack of air support drew strong criticism from the Aussies and Kiwis, who had been through all this so recently in Greece, but they too would have changed their minds if they had known what I was to read later. The RAF were heavily outnumbered and lacking spare parts but, as always, even although the odds were against them, they tried their best. Typical of their dedication was the report that when one of the planes was shot down the crew refused to be evacuated to Egypt. They stayed behind to help the beleaguered garrison.

When we docked, the order was given to disembark at the double and get as much gear ashore as possible before the next air raid. We were scarcely ashore when an air raid started. In Britain the bombing was at a high level and there was usually a gap between the warning and the arrival of the aircraft. The situation now was very different because the warning had scarcely been given when the bombers were overhead. They came down so low that, as they dropped their bombs, you felt that they had you directly in their sights. Although there was little cover, on this occasion the casualties were slight. We unloaded

Suda Bay. Australian and New Zealand troops disembarking.

Photograph courtesy of the Imperial War Museum

Suda Bay...British troops disembarking.

Photograph courtesy of the Imperial War Museum

our equipment as fast as we could in case another attack came quickly, then we marched to the town of Canea where our HQ was stationed.

A large number of the Australians and New Zealanders who had been in the Battle for Greece were evacuated to Crete. I was very sorry for them. They had fought a rearguard action over the mountains of Greece, being bombed and strafed all the way by the Luftwaffe. Those who were now on Crete had been told that they were going back to Egypt for a well-earned rest, but they were diverted to Crete and were going through the mill again. Some of them looked tired, weary and very dishevelled. The rations in Greece were sparse and I gathered that it was even worse on Crete. There was no doubt that the Aussies and the Kiwis, especially the Maoris, had a reputation as fierce fighters. I hoped that they would be given time to recuperate because they were battle hardened and would be a boost for those of us who were not.

Our Section was billeted in a small house quite near to the HQ of Creforce, the name for the Allied Forces in Crete, that was situated on a hill above Canea. The proximity of Creforce and the comings and goings of all the senior staff gave rise to wild speculations about forthcoming actions. We knew that Major General Weston of the Royal Marines was Commander of the MNBDO (the Mobile Naval Base Defence Organisation). I heard later that General Frieberg, a famous New Zealander and a VC of the Great War, was the Commander of Creforce.

The main talking point in our unit was the impending arrival of our Radio Direction Finder cabins. We were puzzled as to why they were not sent in our ship. The subject was never raised and this was another occasion when the lack of information irked me. I assumed that, when the equipment did arrive, we would be attached to the Marines Anti-Aircraft Unit near Suda Bay. I was hoping the equipment would arrive soon to give us some practice before we went into action. A faint hope, the way things were developing. The bombing continued, but had not intensified so much that we could not make preparations for setting up the RDF equipment if it came soon.

Then came news that shattered us. Suda Bay had become so littered with the wrecks of bombed ships that, shortly after our ship ran the gauntlet, the port was closed. Obviously the ship carrying our equipment had either been sunk or it had turned back to Egypt. I couldn't believe it. Maybe I was the Jonah. This was the giddy limit for me in my oft-thwarted desire to be fully prepared for all that the enemy might throw at me. I was short of experience in firearms, then short of experience on the RDF and now, when we were actually in the war zone and action was imminent, we had no equipment.

The equipment was the "raison d'etre" for our presence on Crete. With no RDF cabins we obviously would be on infantry duty. The change in our duty was never confirmed but as we were already on Marine infantry duty I supposed that it was considered unnecessary. A "Sorry, lads, for the cock up" would have been appreciated. I was obviously still thinking like a civilian, and I was not bursting with confidence about matching my old Lee Enfield rifle against the German Spandau machine gun. I would do my best even if it might be a contest of David against Goliath!

Our main activity now was guard duty. We were on the Canea Sea front where a continuous watch was kept, especially at night. The concentration of troops there convinced most of us that, with Greece only a few miles to the North, a seaborne invasion must be expected soon. The swell of the sea, the breakers as they approached the beach, the moon shining spasmodically through the clouds - all gave the illusion of unseen movement.

I was feeling really edgy because peering out to sea in the half-light causes your eyes to play tricks with you. If you look at something long enough, even a big rock, you could swear that it was moving but you are not sure enough to shout a warning. It might be a German landing craft loaded with troops but the problem was that, if you "cried wolf" too often, you became less than popular. On the other hand, if you gave no warning and the blighters suddenly appeared, you certainly would not be flavour of the month. It was a real nervy job.

Daytime duty had one advantage. In the early hours of the morning, before the daily air raid started, we could have a quick swim in the lovely warm, blue Mediterranean. If our nerves were jangling up to now, there came one occasion when they really jumped. We were having a quick wee dip, I had swum out a bit and was floating peacefully on my back. In that position not only were my eyes shut but also my ears were below the water so I did not hear the lads on shore shouting a warning. A fighter had appeared out of nowhere and, as it banked round and descended, the noise was loud enough to alert me. My free style stroke was not too fast at the best of times but I can assure you that the legs were going like wee pistons.

I heard the rat-a-tat of the machine gun as it opened fire. Fortunately it either missed me or it was aiming at a target up on the shore beyond me but I heard the cannon shells rip through the water. As I scrambled up the beach and took cover (a bit late) my legs were shaking, whether from being used like pistons or from shock I don't know. What an epitaph that might have been! Marine Alex Clark: "Killed on Active Service. Shot in the back and up the bottom while retreating at speed from the enemy". This aerial activity and the prospect of invasion soon put paid to the pleasure of a quiet swim in the morning. Leisure and social activity were non-existent, unless you would class playing leapfrog at sea with the Messerschmitt as a leisure activity!

The attack by the Messerschmitt was a one-off event and, although terrifying to careless bathers, it was actually quite amusing. It was soon to be replaced by serious and more devastating events. The bombing of Canea reached such a pitch that it was impossible to move. Every morning the waves of bombers came over. My knees shook and so did the earth. The large planes (I think they were Dorniers) dropped their bombs in a spread from a fair height. There was no dodging that depth of spread-bombing. You made for the best type of cover, closed your eyes, said a prayer and hoped that your bowels and bladder would not shame you. You came out shaking. I learned later that that this spell of bombing was the most intensive of the war.

The other famous plane, the Junkers 87, known as the Stuka or the Dive-Bomber, also played a major part in the attack on Canea. In level flight the Dive-Bomber was slow but its strategy was very different. Instead of a spread-bombing, it released one bomb on a specific target. As the nickname suggests, it went into a very steep dive, so steep that pilots were known to black out at the bottom of their dive because of the speed and force of gravity. During the dive, as it lined up on the target, it released a single bomb. The Stuka had a siren, and when it increased speed it emitted a screaming noise that built up to a terrifying level of ear-splitting intensity. If you were on or near the line of the target, the sight of the bomb and that siren reaching a pitch that pierced your head, made you clamp your hands over your ears and dive for cover. The psychological effect was tremendous, even though the Stuka was assessed by some to be too slow to be an effective bomber.

I shall tell you in a jiffy how, in my case, I had cause to doubt it's alleged inaccuracy. I had even more cause to agree that the Stuka's dive-bombing served to scare the living daylights out of one.

The occasion I refer to was one of the attacks that occurred at the peak of bombing, before the invasion. After a raid there was usually a pause before the next attack. Once the collywobbles subsided, you had to get as much done as possible in the interval. This time the cook decided to prepare a meal well in advance in case the next raid was prolonged. He placed his dixie, a large pot, on a stove on the outside veranda. It was a typical Service utensil, spotlessly clean and shining like a searchlight in the bright sun.

Unexpectedly, a Stuka appeared over the hill and was on a line to pass over our part of Canea. To our horror it began its dive and it seemed to be coming straight at our house. We suddenly realised that the cook's highly polished pan was on a stove out on the veranda. In the reflection of the sun it must been flashing like mad. We could not have signalled our presence more if we had sent a Morse code signal to the Stuka to say: "Here we are, come and get us."

Those of us who were on the roof tried to warn the rest of them in the billet to take cover. That was an instinctive reaction because there was virtually no time to take any action except to dive for cover. Before the Stuka started to flatten out, I saw the bomb leave the undercarriage of the plane. It flashed in the sun like the belly of a silver salmon leaping out of the water and I was sure that it was dead in line with the house. Although falling at a tremendous speed and coming straight towards us, it seemed to be in slow motion. The noise of the Stuka's siren had risen to an ear splitting pitch. I had time only to crouch down behind a small parapet that bordered the flat roof where I shut my eyes and waited for the end to come. You often hear that in a moment like this, many people see their life flashing before them. I didn't. Only the bomb was flashing before me. Then came an enormous thud, followed by a loud sucking noise and, almost simultaneously, a mighty explosion.

The next thing I was aware of was that everything had gone very quiet. I must have passed out for a brief moment because someone was leaning over me, apparently speaking to me, but I couldn't hear him. I was deaf. I could smell the acrid explosive and taste the dust.

We had been lucky. The bomb had narrowly missed the house but the blast had shaken it badly. Fortunately for us the parapet gave us protection from the worst of the blast. Luckily my hearing did come back, but I still suffer pain today. The Cook, showing great dedication to his job and a proper sense of priorities, was delighted to find that, miraculously, his meal was not ruined.

I don't remember how long the relentless bombing continued. Even if some RAF planes had still been on Crete, they would have been massacred. The Luftwaffe had the freedom of the air and, even if more planes in Egypt could have been freed from the war in the Western Desert, the long flight would have made assistance to the beleaguered troops on Crete impracticable.

We continued our guard duty on the seafront at Canea, facing the

Aegean seaboard side of the Island. There was obviously still an expectation that these tremendous bombing attacks could be the softening up process for a sea invasion. The intensity of the air attack pointed to the likelihood of it coming soon. I cannot remember how long the waiting and the bombing went on. The constant running for shelter when the Luftwaffe called on us, praying that your name was not on the next bomb, was beginning to affect morale. If only we could retaliate. If only the RAF was still here to take the Luftwaffe on. If only, if only .....

The Invasion

A bombing raid started early one morning and it was much heavier than normal. When it had passed we stood down from guard but remained on standby on the seafront. Almost immediately the drone of aeroplane engines alerted us and we were surprised at another attack coming so soon after the last one. The memory of the Stuka dive-bombers targeting us was still so strong that our instinctive reaction was to dive for cover. Usually when we heard the sound of planes approaching they were soon overhead but this time there was a delay. I looked up to check whether they had diverted to another target and saw plane after plane approaching us. They were very slow, much slower than the usual Stuka and Dornier bombers. The sound of their engines was also different.

They came nearer but still no sign of bombing. I noticed that a much smaller plane followed close behind each large plane. The first plane was almost above us but still no bombing, so I thought they were heading for Suda Bay. Then suddenly I realised why there were no bombs. The smaller plane had rows of windows and at each window you could see, as clear as if he were sitting on a bus, a soldier clasping a gun. He sat bolt upright and looked straight ahead like an unsociable passenger in a bus. It was a glider being towed!

The sudden and unexpected sight of this air armada and the gliders with these statuesque figures at their windows was shattering. It caught everyone napping, including the officers. No mention was ever made in my hearing about the possibility, far less the probability, of an air invasion. I never heard any discussion about the best way for ground forces to repel an air attack by gliders and paratroopers, no mention either of the strengths and the weaknesses of an attack from the air.

For days we had been standing guard on the seafront awaiting what we thought was an imminent sea invasion while the enemy, armed to the teeth, now appeared literally out of the blue. I was engaged in a trivial task and completely unprepared for the sight that suddenly confronted me. I was so taken aback that I stood gaping and motionless. Others must have been in the same state of shock because it seemed ages before anyone on the ground reacted. It was probably only seconds.

The gliders passed over, probably heading for landing areas to the East of Canea. I heard a voice in the distance shouting: "Gliders, these are gliders, the bastards are here. Shoot, shoot, before they can land and shoot you." After a very brief pause the firing started, mainly with small arms. I rushed up to the billets for my rifle to join in the action but an Officer ordered all the MNBDO Marines to fall in because we had to hold our posts on the Canea beach.

Errol Flynn might have disobeyed orders and shot down the whole armada single-handed. I was only Alex Clark so I marched off with my Unit. Instead of heading for wherever the gliders were targeting, presumably East of Canea and Suda Bay, we went at the double to our posts at the seafront.

Soon many more aircraft passed over Canea but this time not pulling gliders. This wave was carrying hundreds of paratroopers. The shock of the first attack took the ground forces by surprise but this time they were ready. The paratroopers jumped from the planes and floated down so slowly that they were being shot as if they were targets in a shooting gallery. Some described it as being like shooting ducks.

German Paratroopers jumping from plane.

Photograph courtesy of Imperial War Museum.

German glider crashed.

Photograph courtesy of Imperial War Museum

Previously I have sounded disparaging about the 1914 Lee Enfield single shot rifles, but it was the volleys of fire from those rifles that killed hundreds of paratroopers in the first wave of the attack. The bodies slumped as they were hit and limply floated down to earth. I don't recall what my emotions were then but now I think of the vulnerability of these young men, about my age, as they descended into our fire. They must have been so terrified as they jumped out of the plane.

I could go on about the action against the first German air attack but it would be mainly hearsay because, being at the sea front, I was not involved in the initial attack from the air.

When the gliders and paratroopers first appeared, I was sure that, despite our lack of experience, we were about to be put to the test. An ordinary Marine does not expect to be involved in a tactical discussion but it was a puzzled Marine who returned to duty on the sea front at Canea. A Battalion of the Welsh Regiment was also on guard at the Canea sea front. I expected either an NCO or an Officer to tell us why we were back on guard at the beach. Lacking any information, we naturally assumed that the air attack was only a diversion and that the main invasion force would still come from the sea.

Throughout the first day of the air invasion we kept a continuous watch to seaward but at first no enemy attack came. I am not sure of the exact time but I was on night watch and it was dark. Signs of great activity appeared far out to sea. Was this the big event? Suddenly the horizon lit up with beams of light criss-crossing one another. We were all engrossed, the scene unfolding before our eyes. We expected a red alert to be sounded but nobody at our HQ seemed to be concerned. It was obvious that the beams of criss-crossing lights were from searchlights on ships moving towards one another. The beams threw up the shadowy silhouettes of ships. It was too far away to identify anything but suddenly some of the silhouettes were rising in the air and then disappearing. No information was coming through to us so we had no idea what was happening and we assumed that this was the

Maoris performing the Haka.

Photograph courtesy of Imperial War Museum

start of the real (sea) invasion.

The action away out to sea continued. We hoped that it was the Royal Navy attacking and sinking a fleet of German ships. If so, it was just possible that some German ships would survive the naval action, so we kept a sharp look out because landing craft could be approaching at any time. It was a tense night.

We had no sleep and those who went off duty, with their bodies shouting for sleep, tried to stay awake in case the action started. All eyes looked to seaward. No need for the CO to tell us to intensify the watch because of the importance of an immediate warning of approaching vessels.

The action eventually died down and all was quiet. It is still as true today as it was then that the vacuum created by lack of positive information is soon filled by rumour. Before long unfounded rumours began to spread like wildfire and created all sorts of anxiety, tension and fear. Another unknown factor was the state of the battle against the airborne troops on other parts of the Island.

All this time we felt that the Command HQ must still believe that the airborne attack was a diversion and that the seaborne invasion would be the main strike. The long night dragged on and on but after nearly 24 hours since the air attack started, there was still no sign of an invading force. When I went off duty I was struggling to keep my peepers open but the fairy with the magic dust soon won and my eyelids slammed shut with a bang.

When I awoke, dawn was breaking over the White Mountains. Oh! how I wished I was home in Scotland, spending the weekend at the Arrochar Youth Hostel. Instead of looking up to the White Mountains I would be looking up to the Arrochar Alps with the mist-shrouded Beinn Arthur rising high above Loch Long. Beinn Arthur was better known as the Cobbler because the tip of the mountain looked like a cobbler bent over his last.

Although these were not the beloved mountains of my homeland, it was still a beautiful scene that greeted my sleepy eyes as the multi-coloured dawn lit up the Aegean Sea. At least the good news was that there was no sign of an invading force and there was little probability of any action in the daylight hours. Word came later that a single caique (a small boat) with about 20 Germans had landed further up the coast. We had no information as to whether last night was the big invasion or only an exploratory sortie. There might have been an attack further up the coast.

We were still retained on the sea front. The Welch Regiment, an Infantry regiment that you would expect to be invaluable to any heavy fighting going on elsewhere, was also held at the sea front. That seemed to confirm the feeling that a seaborne invasion was still expected. It was maddening not to know.

Plenty of rumours circulated about heavy fighting to the East, at Heraklion and Rhetimo, and to the West, at Maleme Airport. We guessed, therefore, that the Germans must have got at least a foothold of sorts on some of these fronts. It felt to us that ages had passed with no action when suddenly a bombshell (metaphorical rather than literal) hit us. The order came to withdraw across the White Mountains to a fishing village called Sphakia on the South coast.

I could not believe it. Although we had been at Canea throughout the initial airborne attack, I always thought that eventually all the forces around Canea would join up to enter the fray against the enemy. It soon became clear that evacuation, not advancement, was the name of the game. We were absolutely shattered. We had not heard the slightest whisper. The situation had to be very desperate if evacuation was the only answer. Evacuation could only mean that the enemy was advancing and that the Battle was lost. For us it had not even begun. What a shambles our excursion to Crete had been.

A rearguard action was now being mentioned. Perhaps all the Canea forces would regroup somewhere along the route and at last I would face the enemy. The failure of the expected seaborne invasion to materialise, coupled with the orders to withdraw, was incomprehensible to me. Yet another of my "Almosts".

Rearguard Action over the White Mountains - The First Via Dolorosa

If I thought that things so far had not gone as I expected, then I am lost for a description of the ghastly period that followed. We were told the reason why we had to cross the White Mountains. The Navy could not use the main ports situated on the North Coast because the Germans controlled them. The South coast was the only option open to the Royal Navy to have any chance of evacuating the troops.

The fishing villages on the South Coast had no facilities for berthing the ships that the Navy would need for evacuation. They would have to lie off shore and the troops (many thousands of them) would be ferried out, mainly by small rowing boats.

The Royal Navy could only carry out the evacuation at night because the Germans had complete control of the sky. Sphakia, a small fishing village, was chosen as the safest evacuation point. The majority of the troops were stationed in the north and, as transport was not available for the many troops involved, they would have to endure a long and difficult march over the very high White Mountains. The mid-summer temperature would be very high with relatively no shade. Food and water would be scarce and many would have to manage without. The road to Sphakia was really a rough, un-metalled track through mountain passes. A high degree of fitness, stamina, endurance and will to survive would be required.

The fact that most of the troops on the Island were located on the North coast meant a mass exodus. I don't know where all the stragglers came from but already the roads were full of lads who were not under any supervision. This was the type of war situation that made me appreciate even more the value of our early training, particularly the need for discipline. The Marines were fit and disciplined and we marched in formation out of Canea, singing as though we were on a route march. As we passed Suda Bay, the extent of the additional damage since our arrival was apparent. I wondered what the Cretans thought of us leaving them to the mercy of the Germans, notorious for their brutal treatment of the population in occupied nations.

As we passed through the olive groves outside Suda Bay, we were told that a Marine detachment would be left behind to take up positions in the olive groves for a possible rearguard action. Given my feelings about my inexperience with firearms, the irony of my next task made me smile. I thought back to my disappointment aboard ship when a training session on the Lewis gun turned out to be a lecture. I had gained the wrong impression that the gun spent so much time at the stop position that it must be very economical on bullets. I could just see myself telling an approaching German with his machine gun pointed at me: "Hold on a jiffy while I look up the manual to find out the appropriate routine for clearing stops."

I was not feeling quite so light-hearted now because I was given the responsibility for humping the unit's Lewis gun over the mountains. I didn't know whether the responsibility was just for the humping bit or

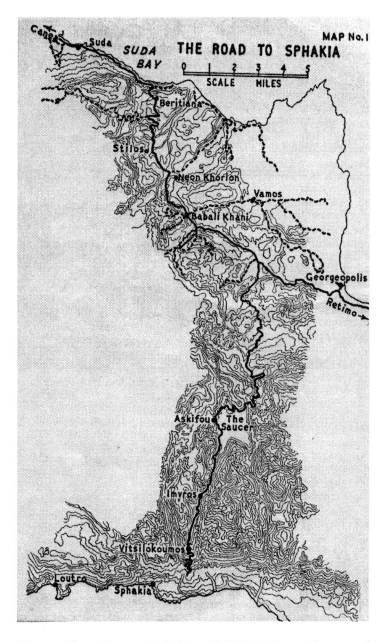

The road from Canea to Sphakia, called 'Via Dolorosa' because of
the horrible conditions of the march.

whether eventually I would be expected to fire the thing. I hoped that my Platoon Corporal, Cpl. Roberts, was a whiz kid with the gun.

We were told that the march from Canea to Sphakia was about 40 miles over mountainous roads and that food, or even water, might not be available. We had to ensure that our water bottles were full and that water should be used very sparingly. It was a bit late to issue that order because the water in my water bottle was conspicuous by its absence. I checked my pack for my "iron rations", a standard issue of hard tack, such as chocolate, contained in a metal tin. It was intended for use on long route marches or for emergencies such as this where food might be scarce. It was gone! Apparently wholesale pilfering had been rife at Canea and I was going to deeply regret my carelessness. It was too late to remedy either the water or the iron rations situation now.

We left the foothills behind and headed up into the White Mountains. I don't know the height of the highest part of the road to Sphakia but I know now that the height of mountains in the range is 2456 metres (about 7500 feet), more than twice the height of a Scottish Munro. As we were still fresh, fit and not too hungry, the pace so far had been good. As we climbed higher there was less shade, the heat of the June sun was taking its toll and the dusty track didn't do much for a dry throat. As far as the eye could see the road was full of men and its narrowness often forced us to march in single file.

On and on we marched and up and up we climbed. I lost all sense of time. It was heads down and try not to think that your throat was burning, your feet swelling and the sweat smarting in your eyes. No question now of singing a marching song.

Do you recall my naïve thoughts on the ship as we approached Crete and these mountains came into view? It was such a beautiful sight with the scattering of small white clouds moving across the tops giving the illusion of the peaks rising slowly into the deep blue sky. When I first saw them, the hills reminded me so much of home that I had hoped to get the opportunity to wander through them, as I so loved to wander through the mountains of home.

Nostalgia swept over me now and for a few minutes my mind was back in the Scottish Mountains. Oh! the joyous memories that daydream brought. On such walks, when the heat became oppressive and the feet swelled up, you stopped at the nearest burn, slaked your thirst and sat on a rock. Off came the socks and shoes and you dangled your toes in the cool running stream. You lay back, closed your eyes and listened to the noise of the water gurgling through the stony shallows. Soon you were floating away in a peaceful snooze.

Fine chance of that now. The fantasy melted like "snaw aff a dyke" and reality took over. Already my mouth was dry and my feet were swollen but I had no burn to dangle my toes in. The track wound its way through the steep ravines and it was dangerous to go too near the edge in case an exhausted soldier, head down and walking in a half sleep, stumbled into you and knocked you over the edge, a drop of hundreds of feet.

The top priority now was to harness all your energies because the main aim was to make it to Sphakia as soon as possible. The probability of a rearguard action could diminish our chances of getting there in time to be evacuated. We appreciated just how difficult it was going to be for the Navy. It could be another Dunkirk but this time there would be no Royal Air Force to give protective cover and no armada of small boats from the Kent coast to help them in their task. The severe threat from the air might compel them to withdraw before all the troops could be evacuated.

Again I looked back in appreciation at our training at Chatham, in particular those punishing route marches, at the end of which you were tired, sometimes exhausted. Your shoulders were sore where the webbing of a full pack had cut in. Your feet ached and, until they hardened, blisters formed. When the barracks hove in sight, the Sergeant inevitably shouted: "Come on, lads, head up, chin in, arms swinging and make those boots hit the ground with a bang. Let them know the best squad is coming home." It was amazing how the aches and pain disappeared as you set your mind to not letting the squad down.

The task ahead made our training marches look like a Sunday afternoon stroll, but those training sessions were still proving their value. The road to Sphakia, later referred to as the "Via Dolorosa", was going to test our endurance to the limit. We were weakened by the lack of food and water, dehydrated by the heat, with limbs protesting strongly at the non-stop grind up those inhospitable hilly roads.

A heart-rending sight was seeing some poor soul, already unable to take another step and finding it all too much for him, lying at the side of the road, utterly exhausted. No amount of pushing, shoving and shouting "Get up, move or you'll be a POW by nightfall" could penetrate a mind equally as exhausted as the body. The plight of these poor lads acted on me like a spur. This was no training march with your head held high before you entered the barracks but the mental process was the same. Lift your head up and concentrate on survival and reaching Sphakia. Forget your aches and pains. If there's a rearguard action ahead of you, just do your best, get through it and then go like hell for Sphakia and that ship bound for Egypt. I know it sounds like Boys Own Magazine now, but it worked.

The road was still winding through the ravines. I don't recall any Messerschmitt at this point but probably the narrow and steep valleys presented too much of a problem for fast planes to manoeuvre. A German spotter plane, probably the Sikorsky (a slow flying plane like the British Lysander) came over frequently. One plane came in so low that it was actually below the level of the road. After so long walking away from the enemy, the first reaction was to open fire, especially at such a slow flying plane. Because of our situation we were under strict orders not to open fire on any enemy plane. We were to get down and not move a muscle – frustration, frustration, frustration; always on the receiving end.

It made sense, however, when we were told the obvious. The function of that spotter plane was to relay information back to the advancing Germans about troop numbers. We could have done with a bit of information too because we knew nothing of what was happening either ahead or behind. If some of our lads had been involved in the rearguard outside Suda Bay, we were desperate to know whether they had survived and were on their way to Sphakia. We should know soon because, if they had managed to disengage from the enemy, they should catch us up when we halted to form the front line for a rearguard action. If they did not catch us up, well we preferred not to dwell on that.

The narrow road with very sharp and steep hairpin bends twisted like a snake through the valleys. On we trudged, eyes down on the road, still trying to obliterate all thoughts of hunger, thirst, heat, sore feet, etc. and to have but one thought in mind, to keep going, to keep going. And when our N.C.O. shook us out of our torpor with a shout: "Take cover", we learned to dive for cover and to freeze, reforming our positions in the march as soon as it was clear.

Trying to keep a reasonable pace in that terrain would have been tough if I had only been carrying my rifle but the heavy machine gun was beginning to feel like a cannon. The weight of it and the continuing lack of water was weakening me. I wondered whether dehydration would make me hallucinate and see a mirage of a lovely cool bubbling burn at the bottom of the valley, just like the French Legionnaires. Just a thought, I wasn't nearly at that stage but there was a time yet to come!

Askifou

I don't remember how many days we had been marching when we entered a plain, sandwiched in between the tips of hills. It seemed quite fertile and we could now leave the narrow road that had made us feel we were on a tightrope with the deep ravines waiting below to catch us. For the first time in ages, the mountains were no longer towering over us oppressively. Now we were out in the open and could take a deep breath.

We had entered a small plain beside a village called Askifou. As

73

expected, whenever we reached an open space we would receive a lot more attention from the German Air Force, who now had an air base at Maleme. The fast fighter planes came over frequently. In the open terrain, surrounded by more gentle hills such as at Askifou, they could come over a hill and dive into the valley in a flash.

We trudged along, eyes down on the road, still trying to obliterate all thought of our condition. I was wishing I had a wheelbarrow for that damned machine gun. The road was still a moving mass of men as we approached the open area around Askifou – "The Saucer" - an apposite nickname for a plain surrounded by hills. The presence of a disciplined force was obvious. A New Zealand Brigade held the position to the North and they had several pieces of artillery. That cheered us up no end. These were the first guns that we had been associated with since the Marine Bofors outside Suda Bay. At least we now had something bigger than a machine gun.

Our Unit left the road and formed up. After so long in confined ravines, no thought except concentration on keeping going, my brain was now in low gear. Yet suddenly it dawned on me that out here in the open, there could be only one reason for forming up. We could hold positions if the enemy tried to outflank us. When the New Zealand Brigade had done their bit, they would withdraw and our position would become the Front Line. This would be our long awaited rearguard action.

When we first left the road at Askifou, it was a pleasure, after all the hot sticky days of humping that damned gun, to lay it down and not have it beside me night and day. My separation from it was all too transitory because I was told to set it up and load the magazines. As I feared, I was not just to be the "humper". I had been elevated to Lewis Gunner. Help, Help!! Send for that Lecturer on the Bergensfjord.

I was not too enamoured of the situation. The German modern Spandau gun versus a 1914 Lewis Gun did not seem a fair match, better than a rifle, however. I was thinking that at last I would soon be confronting the enemy face to face. The thought that I might soon be facing the enemy, less prepared than I would have wished, surfaced again. I wondered if it was a premonition.

I dismissed the pessimistic thought that the German Spandau machine gun had a fearsome reputation and that I had not actually fired the Lewis gun in practice. After all the apprehension about my inexperience, I was amazed that I suddenly was quite calm. Probably embedded somewhere in my brain was the philosophy of "If your name is on the bullet there is nowt that you can do about it".

The Lewis gun was loaded, ready for action and, so as long as it did not jam too much, I had a chance. I was ready for whatever was to come even if I had to tell a scared wee man inside to shut up. To be honest, I was more concerned not to make a pig's ear of it all.

It was now a question of settling down. We would not be involved until the New Zealand Brigade withdrew and passed through our line. I kept squinting down the sights and trying to recall what the lecturer aboard ship told us about freeing stoppages on the Lewis gun. That lecture seemed aeons ago now.

I cannot remember how long we waited for that first warning of the New Zealanders coming through. The fighters were screaming over us more frequently now, perhaps attacking the New Zealanders back up the road. A feeling was in the air that something was about to happen and I felt the tension inside me mounting. Was this the confrontation that I had been waiting for?

They strafed the plain more often now. The fighters were so fast that they were on top of you almost before you heard them approach, the dreaded Stuka had the reputation for inciting the most fear, but I was no longer so sure about that. I recalled the tremendous speed of the Messerschmitt that dived on us in Canea Bay. One like that coming over a hill at high speed and opening up with cannon shells also invoked a fair degree of sensitivity in my bowels. I was very soon going to make a reassessment of the Messerschmitt versus the Stuka competition.

I was still getting familiar with the Lewis gun when an Officer rushed up to our position and said that he needed a courier at the double. "At the double, Clark," shouts my Corporal: "You are the fittest." I am damned if I felt the fittest. When I heard what I had to do, my knees felt very unfit. I was ordered to go up the hill where one of our platoons was holding the left flank of the line. The message was that they were to withdraw immediately because they were in danger of being outflanked by a contingent of the German Mountain Regiment.

I started off, keeping a sharp eye on the valley to my right because that was usually the direction from which the fighters came when they strafed the area between the platoons. I was half way up the hill when one of them came over the hill and screamed up the valley. I was right out in the clear when he opened up and I had only seconds to find cover. I was very lucky. A large rock was just to my left. I dived behind it just as a stream of cannon shells came whizzing past. That was when my bowels and I instantly put the Messerschmitt ahead of the Stuka in the "terror striking" league.

I went up the rest of the slope as quick as my legs would go (You will note that I no longer refer to them as wee pistons). I reached the top, ready to deliver my urgent message but the Platoon must already have anticipated the situation because they had vanished. So I scrambled back down to report, only to find that the Unit was under orders to withdraw and was already assembled, ready to move. Once more I had been ready to confront the Germans and it had not materialised, another of my "Almosts". How many more? I wondered.

Back on the road once more, I had to pick up the Lewis gun and march on. We were really beginning to wilt and I had little idea of the passage of time. The road from Canea to Sphakia was about 40 miles so we must have been marching for days with no water and food. The Saucer was left behind and we were entering the last stretch of the descent to Sphakia. A tailback was forming, presumably because the number of people arriving at Sphakia was increasing far faster than the Navy could evacuate them. Now that the German planes had an air base close by at Maleme, they had complete dominance of the air. The Navy must have been having a very rough time even although they operated only at night. The disturbing rumour was that they might only operate for another night or two.

Soon my circumstances and my long-term future took a disastrous turn for the worse. Our small group of RDF Operators, under Corporal Roberts, was detailed to take charge of an item of technical equipment that must not fall into German hands. This was good news because we were assured of priority on the first available ship. The bad news for me was that the Navy was supposed to be insisting that all personnel had to have a full water bottle. As you know, my bottle had been empty since leaving Suda Bay. Others were in the same predicament.

Away down at the bottom of the very steep valley was a well around which a fair number of men were gathered. I was ordered to go down and get my flask filled. I have been told that one could not march in the conditions of heat and exertion that we suffered without drinking for days. I know that my water bottle was empty when I was in the olive groves outside Suda Bay and it was empty when I was ordered to fill it at that well. I cannot recall drinking in between these places and, if I did, I would certainly have filled my water bottle. With hindsight, sending me down the valley to fill my bottle was not necessary because the Navy would never have refused to take aboard an evacuee because he had no water.

But orders are orders so I scrambled down to the well. Nobody was in charge and the situation was chaotic. An angry group was gathered round a poor Cretan who had told them that the well was poisoned but I didn't wait to hear whether it was or not. I decided that with all that rowdy lot it was going to take a long time to sort things out. If I delayed any longer, the lads would have no option but to move on because troops hanging about were treated very suspiciously. They would expect me to catch them up.

My legs were so weary that I thought that I wouldn't make it up to the road but I did and my worst fears were realised. The lads had gone! All thoughts of weariness disappeared in a flash and I pushed myself down that road as fast as my legs would go. I knew that if I did not catch them up soon, some Officer would stop me to ask why I was not with a unit.

That fear was also soon realised. A Royal Marine Officer stopped me. I told him my tale and whether he believed me or not, I do not know. He ordered me to accompany him back up the hill where once again the Marines, this time with the Australians, had been given the task of holding the final rearguard action. I do not recall seeing the New Zealanders passing through but they must have passed through Askifou and been evacuated. They really deserved it because they had been in the thick of most of the action.

Fate had dealt me a nasty blow because I realised that I had absolutely no chance now of catching up with my platoon. The Officer who brought me back said he regretted separating me from my platoon but he was mustering as many Marines as possible to bolster up the defensive line. My immediate thought was that he was awfully pushed to have to depend on someone of my condition and experience. I was more like a soft pillow than a bolster but I kept the thought to myself.

He told me that the Front was only 2 miles from Sphakia. I realised that if there were a German attack, it could hold us up long enough to make it very difficult to withdraw the two miles down the road to Sphakia in time to catch the last boat to freedom. It was with weary limbs and an empty mind that I plodded my way back up the road to the Front Line.

I had no idea how long it took me. My body was crying out for water and food and above all, for sleep. Utter exhaustion was taking over. I reported to my new Unit, took up my position and lay down. I no longer had the Lewis gun so the Germans had only my trusty Lee Enfield rifle to fear. I tried very hard not to fall asleep but at least I was no longer in danger of being classed as a straggler. I was back with the

Marines again although not with anyone I knew. My RDF comrades must have been wondering what had happened to me and wishing that they had never sent me for water. So was I.

Nearby were the Aussies, a real war hardened bunch of veterans, lads all well blooded in Greece. The defensive line was spread out right across the steep valley so our flanks were covered and any attack from the Germans would have to be down the narrow Pass.

I was desperately trying not to allow my present situation to make me give up all hope of being evacuated at the last minute. Fighting troops were being given priority to board ship when they had finished their stint. Perhaps, when we were ordered to retire, we could move quickly enough to catch the last ship, a pretty slim chance but it was at least something to stop me getting down in the dumps.

My new Sergeant could see that I was on my uppers and he told me that he would look out for me if I just shut my eyes for a wee while. He said with quiet humour that there would be no problem waking up if anything happened. I knew what he meant when I awoke to a series of terrifying explosions. How on earth, I thought, could planes in the half-light see a target deep down in a valley?

The bombing went on for ages and shrapnel was whizzing all over the place. It was another "head down and say a prayer" situation. "What the hell was all that?" I asked my new comrade when the bombardment finished. "That's our special alarm clock for wakening sleepy Marines," he said. "It's called mortar bombs." I was flabbergasted because, having no experience of mortar bombing, I thought that it was a low-level weapon, a bit like a catapult.

I now knew differently. Maybe they were not to be compared to the accuracy and range of the Bofors guns of the Marines but the effect in a situation like ours was devastating. The shrapnel inflicted terrible injuries on personnel. The affect on morale of a heavy mortar bombardment for a long period was shattering, to say the least.

I wondered why the Germans, who were now in much the stronger and more advantageous position, did not attack us. An Aussie, who had experienced rearguard actions in Greece, had the answer. The Germans knew that there were thousands of troops in the Sphakia area, just waiting to be evacuated. They would probably feel that there was no sense in losing men to attack a force that was in a hopeless situation. The mortar attack was just to make sure that we kept our heads down and didn't get any daft ideas of a suicidal counter attack.

The same applied to us. Our objective was just to hold back the Germans long enough to allow as many of our troops as possible to get away, hopefully including us. We were so near Sphakia that we would only attack if forced to, a sensible theory that gave me the hope that after all we might get that last chance to get away.

During this period something happened that provoked very strong feelings, particularly among the Australians. It nevertheless had its humour. We were warned to look out for a Sunderland plane that would be arriving to take off Major General Weston, the Commandant of the Royal Marines. A bonfire was to be prepared on the hill above the defensive line. If it were necessary, when the plane arrived, the bonfire was to be lit as a signal.

This caused uproar from the Australian lines. We had been forbidden to show even a lit match because the Germans would let fly with the mortars at the slightest hint of a light. What would they do if they had a bonfire to light up the whole defensive line? I did not know what the Germans would do but I soon knew what the Aussies would do. An Aussie voice rang out: "That Pommy should be staying to the end. I shoot at the first stupid bastard who tries to light that bonfire."

The Aussies would often say to you: "Good on yer, yer old bastard." They meant it as an expression of friendliness but I fear it was not so intended on this occasion. Fortunately the bonfire was not lit so the Aussie's threat was never put to the test.

Sphakia

Mentally and physically I was just holding on and I cannot say exactly where we were ordered to halt. It must have been just above the beach at Sphakia. A Marine Officer addressed the assembled remnants of the Royal Marines and, although I cannot remember his exact words, the gist of it was as follows:-

"Because the Navy are no longer able to withstand the air bombardment, this will be the last night to evacuate troops. As there are still thousands of troops around Sphakia, it will be impossible for all to be evacuated. The GHQ in Cairo have left orders that fighting troops be given priority but regretfully, it is now probable that not all of you who were involved in the last rearguard action can expect to be given priority for evacuation. I suggest that, as you are all in a state of complete exhaustion, you lie down and sleep. Some of you may be awakened and will be evacuated. Those of you who sleep through until morning will know that regrettably you will not be evacuated. Tomorrow morning the Island of Crete will be officially surrendered from GHQ Cairo."

I had half expected that I was fated to be left behind. My ever recurring "Almost Syndrome" may have prompted that negative thought. I still clung to the belief that the Marines in charge of the evacuation down at Sphakia, would do all in their power to ensure that the Marines who were involved in holding the line to the end would not be left behind. The Officer was right about our falling asleep. Despite the awful prospect that I might not be one of those to be awakened, my weary body was immediately overcome by sleep. All I can remember before the blessed sleep took over on that terrible night was that the ground was covered in big stones and that I had to make a hole for my hip.

The next thing I knew was that it was daylight. I was still dopey with heavy sleep. It took a few seconds before it dawned on me that I was awake, it was daylight and it was not a nightmare, it was reality. I had not been awakened and I was still on Crete. I had not been selected to join the last ship off the island. I was left behind.

I don't know to this day how the most important selection of my life to date was made. A selection that determined whether I would be free or be facing incarceration for God knows how long. A mind-boggling confusion of emotions rushed through my mind and even today, so long after the event, I find it difficult to express them in meaningful words. At first I found it unbelievable that I was actually left behind.

From the day that War was declared I had prepared myself for the worst and I accepted that I could be wounded and even that I might be killed. The Marines' training strengthened my approach to accepting that philosophy. When I arrived in Crete, I felt physically and mentally in good shape. I had all the optimism of a young man, 20 years old, so that I could cope with all the situations that arise in battle. I had accepted the Marines' culture of team spirit and regimental pride – never let the Regiment down. Of all regiments, how could the Marines have left us behind? How could they, especially my comrades in the RDF Unit, have sailed away and know that they had left me behind?

At no time did anyone ever prepare us for, or even mention to us, the possibility of being in the ghastly situation that we were in now. Thus we had not been prepared to cope with it. I felt deserted, humiliated, disgusted, disoriented. None of these words come anywhere near to truly describing my emotions in what was one of the worst moments in my life. It was very difficult not to succumb to feelings of deep depression. The worst yet of my many "Almosts".

Now, so long after the event, I know how unfair some of these thoughts were. I realise that it would have been utterly unacceptable to expect my comrades to refuse to board the last ship. It would have been a futile and stupid gesture. For all they knew, I might have been a fatal casualty. I did not know then the difficult situation at the evacuation point. I certainly did not know the terrible sacrifices, the

Royal Navy destroyer approaching rowing boat with troops being evacuated.

Photograph courtesy of Imperial War Museum

loss of life and ships that the Navy had suffered in trying to uphold their traditions in rescuing troops from such situations. As they sailed away on that last fateful night in June 1941, they must all have gone through hell as they looked back at the thousands left behind.

In the New Zealand film production Touch and Go, about the Battle of Crete, there is a scene showing what was probably the last ship to leave Sphakia. A few men are leaning over the side of the ship looking back to the shore. One of them had a haunted look in his eyes. I am almost certain that he was Corporal Roberts of the Royal Marines, the same Cpl. Roberts who sent me down the valley to fill my water bottle. That Marine had the look of a man going through hell. If it was Cpl. Roberts, I am sure that the haunted look was due to the fact that he had left me behind.

I never again saw any of my comrades in the RDF Unit. Some of them were killed at Tobruck and Cpl. Roberts might have been one of them. I am sad if that is so, if not, then I hope that he is alive and well. I assure him that had I managed to get down to the shore at Sphakia on that unforgettable night when he sailed away, I would have waved goodbye and wished him well, probably with a tear most unbecoming for a hardened Marine.

Evacuation scene at Sphakia

Photograph courtesy of Imperial War Museum

Evacuation scene at Sphakia

Photograph courtesy of Imperial War Museum

Chapter 6

Capitulation

Crete Surrendered

A young Royal Marine Lieutenant was walking round awakening all the Marines who had been left behind. He told us that, on Orders received from Cairo, the Island had been officially surrendered and everyone had to lay down their arms. I was sorry for the young lieutenant because he too must have been suffering something he had never dreamt off. I admired the way that he was taking charge and trying to think clearly what action to take. He formed up the Marines, marched us down to the beach, and stressed again that the Island had been officially surrendered by the GHQ in Cairo and, no matter what our feelings on the matter, we were under orders to dispose of all firearms and ammunition.

I stood for a moment on the ledge, watching the waves breaking at the entrance of the cove and then running up and down the sides, a peaceful scene on a lovely summer day. In another time you could sit down and allow the lapping waves to wash away your worries. I threw my old Lee Enfield rifle far into the sea. As it sank below the surface, I had mixed feelings. I wrote earlier of my concern when I knew that I, a non-violent person, would soon be going to war and that I could be aiming that rifle at someone whom I did not even know with the intention of killing him. As soon as I joined up I knew that, if the occasion arose, I would use my rifle, even if the sight of the dead man that I had killed lived with me for the rest of my life.

I had pushed these thoughts away, deep down. As I watched the bubbles burst over the spot where my rifle sank, I reflected that it had been by my side for over a year now. On pain of dire punishment if I failed to look after it properly, I had kept it scrupulously oiled, kept it clean – nay, absolutely spotless, and carted it around half the Hemisphere. I had trembled when I was chosen on parade or on route march to have my rifle examined. The Sergeant would lift the rifle to the skies and squint up the barrel while I held my breath in case he spied a minuscule particle of dust.

Within the last week or so I was ready, on several occasions when I confronted the enemy, to let it fulfil its purpose in life. Alas, on each occasion we were withdrawn because the Germans chose to stand back. The poor wee thing, its purpose in life unfulfilled, was now committed to a watery grave. I thought it was strange that, despite my earlier feelings on the subject and the rifle's inactive career, I now felt quite naked and defenceless without it, a daft feeling hardly justified by the loss of a rifle that really should not have survived the First World War.

The feelings of disgust and humiliation welled up again. After all the effort made by everyone to do their best in the terrible conditions we had endured in the last few weeks, we were now reduced to this. We then took cover in a rocky inlet and sat down wearily to await a fate no longer in our own hands.

Captured

I sat listening to the waves lapping up the sides of the rocky cove and trying to come to terms with my present state. I thought again how ill-prepared we were to cope with the trauma of the events leading up to surrender and of becoming a prisoner of war. At no time had there been any training or even any advice given in preparation for this eventuality. To my knowledge there was never even a mention of how to cope with the situation that now faced us.

Did the young Lieutenant in his training discuss the possibility of managing hundreds of men who had been ordered to surrender and awaited the arrival of the enemy? Did anyone back home consider the immediate problems of the aftermath of surrender now facing him?

These men were now possibly facing incarceration for years as POW's. Perhaps the possibility of capture was an unmentionable subject in the military mind but in our case, to surrender or not to surrender, was not a personal decision. The order came from the very top.

I stood on the ledge listening to the sound of the waves, a peaceful and quiet scene it might have been, but an uneasy quiet and I certainly did not feel at peace. When we were on the rearguard action there had been tension in the air and also a fair degree of apprehension and fear. However we had been armed then, now we were defenceless. We could only sit and wait, with considerable trepidation, for the arrival of the Germans.

How would they act? If they had no knowledge of the official surrender, they might expect us to resist to the end. In that case they might shoot on sight. It could be a massacre.

We kept a wary eye on the cliff top above us. Eventually a few heads poked ever so gingerly above the edge. Then the Spandau machine guns were levelled at us. We held our breath as the young Lieutenant walked out into the open. If our pulses were beating fast, his must have been racing like mad. He shouted "Hande Hoch" (Hands up). That took some courage.

What thoughts must have gone through his head? I knew that phrase 'Hande Hoch', from the Hollywood films of the Great War. For me it symbolised the shame and humiliation of surrender. Yet why should I have felt shame and humiliation? I was only a pawn on the gigantic chessboard of war. Someone up there moved the pawns around until the moment came when they had to be discarded to protect the Kings and Queens. When that young Lieutenant had been commissioned, he probably had had thoughts of leading his men courageously, had dreams of victory.

Now he had the task of leading his men, courageously without doubt, not into battle but into captivity. His disillusionment must have known no bounds.

I have suffered many lapses of memory. What happened next is one of the greatest. I can remember the Germans appearing on the hill above us. I can recall the intense feelings of misery and despair as I started the climb up the cliff and into the gorge that led to the village of Vitsilokumous.

The steep cliff was too much for some. Men began to fall by the wayside, some to die, others just too exhausted to take another step. What happened to them? I don't know because we were pushed on. The climb up was slow and in our condition it felt like the end of an assault on Everest. I have no memory from that time until we reached the olive groves outside Canea, almost 40 miles away.

Many times during the last 58 years, I have looked back over that period and concentrated my mind to try to bring memories up from the depths. I thought as I started to write about it something might stir, but nothing surfaced*.

Nowadays psychiatrists tell us that the mind can bury unpleasant memories completely. Certainly the march along that ghastly stretch of road from Suda to Sphakia was horrific yet for most of it I can now recall nothing. The return journey was over the same road but the circumstances made it immeasurably worse. When I knew that I had been left behind on that awful morning on the cliff above the evacuation beach at Sphakia, I felt that I had plumbed the depths of hunger, thirst, exhaustion and despair. But more, much more was yet to come.

[* See Appendix G – "In Search of Lost Memories"]

The March Back over the Mountains
– Via Dolorosa the Second

I heard later that a few men, who were still reasonably fit, decided to escape into the mountains in the hope that Cretans would be able to keep them under cover. But the majority of the thousands left behind, lying around the Sphakia beaches or hiding in coves, were unfit and far too exhausted to even contemplate an escape to the mountains. Many indeed were hospital cases and would be unable to survive the rigours of the march back over the second Dolorosa.

In any event, escaping to the hills was feasible only if a handful undertook it. The German troops rounded up the broken Allied forces and we began the long and even more horrendous march back over the mountains.

The long lines of men who climbed up the steep road that led from the Sphakia beach to Vitsilokoumos had reached the nadir of misery. They were even hungrier, thirstier and more exhausted than they were on the march to Sphakia. Added to all their sufferings there was now the deep, deep feeling of humiliation.

Morale was not just very low, it was non-existent. This time there was no stepping out, no hope, no respect, and no prospect. On the way to Sphakia they had forced themselves on despite all the physical and mental tortures. Then, no matter the difficulties on the road ahead, they had the motivation of picturing in their mind a ship just over the horizon, waiting to take them to safety and freedom. Motivation was now replaced by empty despair.

These German soldiers, the first of many wardens of the long and accursed incarceration to come, herded them like cattle. The guards were obviously under orders to press on and get this mass of humanity off Crete quickly and back to Germany. I learned later that the urgency was because Adolf Hitler wanted to open the Eastern Front before the onset of winter and he needed as many troops as soon as possible.

For us it was now just a case of staying alive and at times even that did not seem worth it. Again my mind must have drawn the curtains because I do not remember passing the three places where events had had such a big influence on what happened to me. The first was Vitsilokoumos, just outside Sphakia, where I was involved in the last rearguard action. The second place was where I went down for water and became separated from my RDF Unit.

The third place was at Askifou, 'The Saucer', where we were preparing for a rearguard action and where the Messerschmitt fighter plane strafed me. If I had no memory of passing these places, then my mind must have gone into automatic pilot. Perhaps I was suffering from the complaint much mentioned today, post-traumatic syndrome.

Although I was oblivious to my surroundings for most of that march, I knew that I was deteriorating physically by the hour and I have no idea how many days were spent in traversing that second "Via Dolorosa". All I tried to do was to keep my eyes on the road and try not to think about the immediate future or indeed about anything at all.

If it actually was a withdrawal from reality during the march (and not just an elderly man's later loss of memory) then I suppose that I was really lucky. The future was non-existent and the present was so horrific that my determination to survive was being sorely tested. It was not until we came down from the mountains into the olive groves before Suda Bay that my mind dramatically jerked back to reality. A smell hit my nostrils with intensity such as I had never before encountered, the overpoweringly sweet and sickly smell of death. I had occasionally come across the decaying body of a sheep but this smell was so much more powerful.

I realised that we had reached the olive groves outside Suda Bay where one of our Marine detachments had been left behind on the outward march. The cause of the smell came soon into sight and a horrible sight it was. Obviously a rearguard action had taken place here. Our comrades, who only a short time ago had been part of our life, who were young and active with all their life ahead of them, were still leaning on the trees they had used for cover. After a long time in the tremendous heat their bodies were black and putrefying, I don't know how long rigor mortis lasts but their arms still held their rifles in the firing position as if stiffened in death. I was overcome with sadness and sickened by the smell.

Although identification was difficult as we marched past, I was almost certain that the nearest body was that of a Royal Marine. I was stunned. But for the Grace of God, I could have been lying there. I felt bad that I was not sure whether or not they were our lads who had been left behind to hold the Line. Once again it was driven home to me how, in a war situation, someone at my level knew so little of what was happening around him.

I pointed to the corpse and indicated to the Guards that we wanted to identify the bodies of our comrades and to give them a burial before we left them behind. An NCO rushed up, made a digging action, pointed to some Cretans and angrily waved us on. I felt very low. I was hit very hard both by coming so suddenly on that horrible sight and by the refusal to let us bury our own dead.

Only a short while ago I had been bemoaning my lot at being left behind at Sphakia. I now felt ashamed as I walked away from the blackened corpses that such a short time ago had been our young fit and strong comrades. I was alive but they would never see home again. I forgot, for a moment, my weakened body screaming for food, water and rest. I felt a sense of guilt as I turned to go, leaving them behind forever*.

If we were going by sea to Greece, it was obvious that we would go first to Suda Bay. The only incident that I can recall for the rest of the march was seeing a field of turnips. I had been trying not to let the desperate hunger keep dominating my thoughts but these mundane

[*I saw their graves in 1998. See Appendix G.]

93

turnips looked like manna from heaven. Breaking ranks was very dangerous, but hunger clouds the senses so I made a quick dash into the field and returned with the treasure before the guard turned round. I only had a couple of bites before the turnip was snatched away from me. It disappeared in a flash as though a shoal of piranha fish had descended on it.

That was the first morsel of food that had passed my mouth in a very long time. We arrived at Suda Bay and the Cretan part of our "Via Dolorosa" was over. As we stood on the quay it was difficult to realise that the poor emaciated specimens of humanity we were now were the same men who had disembarked at this very spot. The same men who were fighting fit and hoping to succeed in whatever lay ahead. Without delay we were rushed onto a small ship tied up at the quay. It would convey us on the next stage of a very long and horrific journey to Germany.

Chapter 7

Greece

Piraeus and Salonika

I don't recall much about the journey to Greece but the small ship was most likely a cargo vessel. It certainly was not designed to accommodate people. We were packed like sardines into an area that looked like a hold, with no water, no toilets and no seats. I sat on the deck, curled up in a corner. The disaster of Crete was behind me and at least I had survived. God only knows what disasters lay ahead.

They battened down the hatches and as darkness descended I heard the engines starting up and the ship got under way. For a long time we moved slowly, probably because Suda Bay was so full of damaged and sunken ships that navigating a way through them would be difficult. The ship picked up speed and began to rise and fall with the swell of open sea. The view to the South should have been the same that greeted me as we had approached Crete, the White Mountains rising up through the clouds into the blue sky.

The view might have been the same but my situation was so very different. The hold was packed with men leaving Crete but not sailing to freedom in Egypt, the motivation that had kept them going on the Via Dolorosa. They were headed for an unknown destination in Nazi Germany.

Normally it would have been noisy with so many men in an enclosed space but it was strangely quiet. Most were exhausted and sleeping. I know that my mind was in a whirl and I couldn't think straight. When I described sitting in that inlet in Sphakia, waiting to surrender to the German soldiers, I struggled for words to describe my emotions and feelings. The situation now was infinitely worse but I've used up all the superlatives.

I was filled with despair and, I must admit, a real anxiety about what sort of life might be awaiting me. I indulged in a spell of self-pity, an emotion that I have always detested. If only I hadn't gone down that ravine to fill my water bottle, I could now have been in Egypt. I even entertained thoughts that fighting and dying beside my comrades in the rearguard action outside Suda Bay might have been preferable to my present plight.

Then I gave myself a good mental shaking because deep, negative thoughts about the future did not help me one bit. Anticipation was often worse than reality. I decided at least to try to think positively instead of, as at present, dwelling morosely on the events in the Battle of Crete. Gradually the effects of exhaustion again took over. Disturbing emotions, jumbled thoughts and fears, floated away into the oblivion of blessed sleep.

I knew no more until I awoke to the noise of the ship's engines reversing. We were entering Piraeus, the port of Athens. We disembarked and were bundled immediately into a horse box type of railway wagon that, by comparison, made the hold of the ship from Crete seem commodious. Everything was being done at breakneck speed as the Germans continued to push us on. We were packed in tight, sitting shoulder to shoulder with hardly room to breathe.

Toilets and other essential facilities were not a built-in feature of railway horseboxes. I don't know how many horses it was supposed to accommodate but we were scarcely in a position to mount a protest about the number of humans in it. We didn't feel like humans anyway. It wasn't long before we entered the beautiful city of Athens and I recalled again my teacher at school stressing the value of a visit to Athens and Mount Olympus for a real appreciation of ancient Greek culture.

I wasn't over enthusiastic about Greek history at that moment in time but as the train slowed down going through Athens, I managed to catch a passing glimpse of the Acropolis. My first sight of the ancient edifice was through a wee window, just above head height and enclosed with the now familiar square of barbed wire. It provided the only ventilation and light available and I had to jump up to see out of it. I was only fit for a couple of jumps and by the time I had recovered from them the Acropolis and Athens had disappeared. If I had a photograph of that glimpse, you would have agreed that it was both ironical and laughable because the Athenaeum would have been etched behind a square of the barbed wire, not quite the scene envisaged by my classics master.

A change of guard had taken place since leaving Crete. The soldiers who took charge of us at Sphakia were front line troops. Although they pushed us hard on that journey, you felt that they at least had some appreciation of our dire situation and maybe a modicum of respect and pity for us, perhaps even an attitude of "There but for the grace of God, go I".

The guards who took charge of us in Salonika were a very different type. They were brutal and sadistic. They gave the impression that they had been trained specifically as jailers and would batter a man for no reason at all except sadistic satisfaction. As you would expect, the weak were most at risk. Stories of brutality by the Germans to people in the occupied countries were legend, so I decided that I would be careful not to protest, at least not while we were so vulnerable.

The train made its way slowly up the coast of the Aegean Sea and I thought back to only a few weeks ago when we looked out over that sea from the south, waiting for the "Sea invasion that never was". As the train progressed up Greece, I recall seeing a name, Larissa, on a railway station. Soon after that the train unexpectedly stopped. A high mountain towered above us. I assumed it was Mount Olympus.

The physical effects of jumping up to squint through a wee square of barbed wire at the Acropolis had rather blunted my enthusiasm for further enhancing my skimpy classical education. I was not in any condition physically, or intellectually for that matter, to jump up to view the home of the ancient Greek gods.

The guards wanted us out of the train at the double and they were running along the train, shouting in their usual panicky state that was becoming familiar. It was more than just impatience. It held the threat that failing to respond immediately would result in severe punishment and, depending on the circumstances and how blood crazy the guards were, that punishment could be fatal.

The Germans' desperation to push us on drove them mad if anything interfered with that objective. The guards went in a perpetual fear of punishment if an Officer or NCO decided that they were slacking. If they wanted us out of the horsebox in a hurry, they shouted and prodded us in the back with a gun, a method they had used from the moment we left Sphakia. It was clear on this occasion that they intended to use the gun, if necessary.

They shouted words we did not know: "Ausmachen, weiter, weiter, schnell, schnell". We responded like a dog that knows what you want by the tone of your voice. It was a great relief to be out of the horsebox for a spell because most of us were feeling the effects of the prolonged period on little or no food and often little water. Many had stomach and bladder problems and a few were showing signs that the dysentery bug was spreading. The air in the horsebox was foul and the clothes of a few poor souls were soiled with excrement. Would any of us, when we were called up to the forces, have remotely envisaged a situation like this?

I thought that we were being allowed a brief respite from our cesspool and that perhaps some of the worst affected might be given medical attention. To my amazement, the guard pointed to the train and said: "Zug Kaput", (Train broken down). Then he pointed to Mount Olympus and said: "Marsch, marsch". It didn't need an interpreter to tell us what that meant. Oh God, I thought, not another Via Dolorosa over mountains, surely not in our very reduced state.

I remember so little of that walk that I can't say how far it was, how long it took or whether any of the lads didn't make it. In other circumstances I would have been delighted to be able to walk up Mount Olympus and soak up the classical environment but I was too preoccupied with survival to bother about that!

It wasn't so long ago (on the march over the White Mountains) that I had realised that my mind going into automatic mode and creating blanks in my memory might be a result of my determination to survive. This was another occasion when my mind decided not to accept another period of strain. The thought of another climb on mountain roads literally put the fear of death into a number of the men who were now quite ill.

Although I was not as bad as some of the lads, I was still not well enough to be other than very apprehensive that I could survive another walk. I know that we set out to walk from that broken down train but there must have been a road alongside the railway because the next thing that I remember is arriving by train at our next destination, Salonika.

I must have been unwell enough to be taken to a hospital on arrival because my next clear memory is of sitting in a waiting room, feeling like death warmed up, in the company of a number of POW's. My stomach was painful, I was shivering like a jelly and I could not stop scratching my armpits and other more sensitive areas.

The lad beside me was apparently knowledgeable on causes of the scratching because he said in a very matter of fact way: "You've got lice, look under your oxters". He was right. My worst affliction from these wee beasties had happened when I was a boy. My Mum found something in my hair and I immediately became the object of intense activity, scrubbing, washing and combing to eradicate the lice, but I don't remember the wee beasties themselves.

The doctor in Salonika examined me and decided I had a mild form both of malaria and dysentery. Other men needed further hospital treatment but the Germans were insisting that only the worst should be retained so he gave me quinine for the malaria and pills for the dysentery and discharged me. I was escorted back to the train.

With so many sick men and under pressure from the Germans, the doctors had the thankless task of deciding who should stay and who should be sent back to the train. The horsebox carriages were still our mode of transport. There were a number of newcomers in our wagon and some of the original occupants were missing, hopefully retained in hospital for treatment. I feared for them because they had been pretty far gone. Had they been treated and returned to the train, I doubt whether they would have survived the next stage of our journey.

I was still feeling poorly but I was fortunate that the dysentery had eased off and the malaria was only giving me occasional bouts of shivering; otherwise I doubt whether I would have survived the journey. Others were less fortunate. Their dysentery worsened and the atmosphere became abominable. What surprised me was that we seemed to acquire a degree of tolerance to conditions that would have been absolutely intolerable in normal circumstances. Was it the instinct for survival or were we just too weak to bother?

I have heard of a punishment where prisoners are locked up in an enclosed space in darkness for a prolonged period of time. The victim loses track of the passage of time and becomes completely disoriented. We were not in darkness in our wagon but the scarcity of light from the little square at the top of the wall and the cramped conditions had a similar effect.

The rhythmic sound of the wheels passing over the gaps in the track and the lack of any other diversion had a soporific, even a hypnotic affect. The only time we had any idea of where we were and of how far we had travelled was when we entered a station. In a normal passenger train the scenery passes by so quickly that it is often difficult to focus long enough to enjoy something that interests you. You can imagine how difficult it was to identify anything of interest through that little square, our window to the outside world. The space in the horsebox was so limited that not everyone could lie down at the same time.

A block of wood was placed below the window so we could look out without need of the jumping up that sapped your energy. In the daylight hours, there was usually someone looking out. We passed through Yugoslavia but I must have been asleep when we went through Belgrade station. I did manage a wee keek out of the window when we stopped for a time in Budapest.

I was interested to learn that Buda and Pest were actually two places, one on each side of the river Danube. The typical humour of the British squaddie is well known, if not always appreciated. Despite the detestable conditions in the wagon, an incident on Budapest station provided us with an example of British humour in adversity. It was our first light-hearted moment since we had left Salonika and it had us all in stitches.

On the platform opposite the train stood a soldier dressed in the most magnificent and gaudy uniform. He could have been straight out of an Operetta and, if he had burst forth into an aria from Gilbert and Sullivan, we would not have been a bit surprised. The long jacket was bright blue with white facings, a white and gold belt glistening in the sun and red and green breeches, spotless above a pair of knee boots so polished that you could see your face in them.

He stood motionless except for looking up and down at the train on the other platform, his hands behind his back, his head held high, his big chest stuck out but not nearly as far out as his even bigger belly. He did look like a General. Just then the General moved. Maybe his troops were advancing up the platform for inspection. His hands came from behind his back, he waved a green flag and the train started to move. Heavens above, he was a railway guard. If he has an outfit like that, what on earth do the generals wear?

That, sadly, was the last light-hearted incident. We were getting weaker, losing all interest in the world around us and most of us lay curled up and asleep. Although sleeping was the best way to conserve energy, you had to stand up sometimes, if only to let someone else lie down. We must have passed through Austria and the romantic city of Vienna but I was asleep. Had I been awake, my weakened body, starved and ridden with fleas and lice, was hardly in a condition to respond to the sound of a Strauss waltz.

I had completely lost sense of time. When the train stopped we were not in a railway station, we were in a siding. The cries of "Ausmachen", and "Schnell, Schnell" rang out again so we knew this was not a normal stop. It was the end of the line.

A guard shouted "Dresden" but I could see no sign of habitation so I assumed that Dresden was nearby. A train journey that started in Athens, called at some of the most famous cities in Europe and finished in Dresden, sounds as romantic as the Orient Express. Instead it had been a longer and more horrific journey that I could ever have imagined.

The relief when I staggered off that train was immense. I sucked in the fresh air. Oh how sweet it was after all that time in the dank horsewagon with the smell of urine and excrement! I wouldn't say that there was exactly a spring in my step. No question of showing the Germans who watched us disembark, the sight of a Royal Marine marching with arms swinging and shoulders back. I was far too trachled and too busy scratching. The lice were breeding fast and they now had the company of fleas.

Part 3

In Durance Vile

Chapter 8

Czechoslovakia

Stalag IVB

We left the train, presumably now en route for the final destination of this horrible journey. Unexpectedly a huge gate, decorated with a mass of barbed wire, loomed up in front of us. Even now when I see barbed wire I feel a twinge. As I walked up the road towards these huge gates, the dreadful reality hit me that I could be encircled by that barbed wire for a long time. I had committed no crime but I would be incarcerated in a prison just like any criminal. The difference was that my sentence was not finite.

An overwhelming fear of incarceration was created then and it has stayed with me ever since. The word fear does not describe it. Neither does the word hatred. The feeling was perhaps similar to the feeling that a criminal under a sentence of life imprisonment must have when the gates of his jail close behind him. It was more like the butterflies in your stomach when you are confronted with something that sets your nerves on edge, something that you have never encountered before and you pray that you will have the strength to cope with it.

The gates and all the fencing around them seemed to rise up above me presenting a sea of impenetrable barbed wire. Two guards were positioned at either side of the gates and beyond them a high barbed wire fence dominated an array of huts. Towers with searchlights were positioned at intervals around the perimeter from which guards with machine guns looked down menacingly.

This was a very large camp called Stalag IVB. Stalag is an abbreviation of Stammlager, a main camp. As we waited for clearance, I felt a knot in my stomach and I was again overwhelmed with that powerful fear of incarceration.

As the gates closed behind me I looked up at the menacing towers, at the guards with their sub-machine guns then - inside the barbed wire fence - at the POW's, who all had that look of resignation of animals in the zoo. It was only then that I fully realised I was now a prisoner. To me these were the gates of Hades and I could have turned and run, such was the strength of my emotion. There is no doubt that I would have been shot and I quickly realised that I was allowing my emotions to take control of me.

I did not run. Instead my self-respect drained out of me. My head went down and my spirit sank lower. I suppose that, however unjustified, I was still feeling a sense of shame that I had been reduced to this after all the years that I had endeavoured to better myself. Prison camp meant goodbye to freedom and it might be forever. For a brief moment I descended again into that self-pity I loathe so much. I thought: "What have I done to deserve this?"

This abhorrence of being closed in remains with me still and I have had many nightmares since the War. I still wake up in a sweat after my worst nightmare. I am in another war and I am once more a POW. The feeling of relief on waking is intense.

The guard brought his gun up to his hip in that menacing position of readiness and whisked us away. That our verminous state was plainly obvious was evidenced by the care everyone took to keep us at a distance. When you knew that you smelled so bad that a skunk would turn and run, it was difficult to be offended.

We were shown into a large building. I don't know what I was expecting but the sight of a row of showers met my eyes. I hadn't seen a shower or a bath since I left Canea. I would have rushed in immediately but certain obvious formalities had to be attended to. We removed our clothes and threw them into huge bags, no doubt to be burned. My clothes were so full of wee beasties that, if the guards had spoken nicely to them, they would have carried the clothes away and saved the expense of burning.

I could have stayed under the shower for hours but we moved on quickly to the next stage of the delousing process. We then entered a room where a number of barbers set upon us with great gusto. They made the Royal Marine barber look like a stylist in a London West End Hair Salon. I was shorn like a sheep until I was as bald as a coot. ALL parts of the body were then sprayed with delousing fluid and some of the more sensitive parts, not having been treated like that before, stung like mad. Notwithstanding all this, that shower was one of the most satisfying and sensuous feelings of my life. What a joy it was, after the weeks of filth and degradation.

The rest of the introduction to POW life obviously could not live up to that. Another symbol of my change of identity was the metal disc that had to be kept round your neck at all times. I was no longer Marine Clark, CHX 100651. I was simply number 95969.

I passed a mirror on the way out and got a shock. A thin and haggard, dehumanised person with a shaved head and an unshaven chin now faced me. I smiled at the apparition and it smiled back. I recognised the smile. It was still me, though I would not have been surprised if my reflection had recoiled in shock. I had to admit that my appearance was so bad that having a number instead of a name seemed quite appropriate. I was used to shouting out my Marine number, now I had two numbers to remember.

When we were finally ushered to our billets, I lay on my bed and pondered my lot. I gave myself a mental bollicking. What had happened to my survival philosophy? Where was the approach of the "head up and look to the horizon when all this is at an end philosophy?" I fell into a sound sleep and awoke in a slightly better frame of mind. Then my eye caught sight of that damnable barbed wire.

The size of the camp surprised me. There seemed to be so many POW's and so many guards to look after them. I was puzzled at the absence of Officers until I learned that Officers spent the rest of their POW career in an Oflag, a special camp for Officers only. Our stay in Stalag IVB was brief. Most of our intake were in no physical state to do any heavy work, at least until we had recovered from our exertions of the past few weeks. Nevertheless a number of us, about thirty or so, were told that we would be sent to a working camp in the next day or so.

Since becoming POWs back in Crete, we had been on the move all the time and I had concentrated so much on just surviving that I had no time to think about what life would be like in a prison camp. That night was the first time in weeks that I had actually spent the night in a building. As we were escorted to our hut, I was still so conscious of that ring of high and thick barbed wire around me. The towers around the perimeter loomed over everything. A guard held his submachine gun at the ready as if he were willing someone to make a break and give him an excuse to use it.

The lads who had been there for some time seemed to pay no attention to the guards but I was very aware that I was now a prisoner. I called it the awful incarceration syndrome. It never left me. The POW's called it "barbed wire madness", a more apt description.

A number of the POW's in the Stalag had been captured at Dunkirk in June 1940. Over a year in this hell hole and they still remembered vividly how they felt on their first night in a prison camp. They were very understanding, chatting to me well into the night about life in a POW camp. I cannot say that it made me feel at ease but I learned a lot that helped me when I went to a working camp.

One lad in particular gave me tips about how he coped with many of the problems that I would meet. An important point was that I must never react to anything that I felt was unjust. Some guards would provoke you deliberately so that they would have an excuse to punish you. There were no appeal courts or trade union officials so you just had to stomach it. He said that the work might be heavy. He advised that, although we were definitely not fit, we should never refuse to do anything. He said: "They either won't understand or don't want to understand. If it is a heavy item, try to lift it and then drop it as though it was accidental. Keep dropping it and then collapse." I thought at the time that he was a bit of a Bolshie but I kept his advice in mind.

I lay awake for a long time that night. Life was going to be so different and adjusting to accept it was going to be difficult. It crossed my mind that I had had very similar thoughts when I sat down on my bed on my first night in the Royal Marine barracks in Chatham. I had to hold fast to the belief that this was only a temporary phase in my life, although it was of an indeterminate duration. No matter the circumstances I would try to project my mind to the day when I would walk free. It was not easy to do at this early stage and it was to become very difficult a few years on.

On arrival at Stalag IVB I had the first experience of that very strong emotion, homesickness. It came when I was handed a pre-printed card to send home. It gave only the bare details that I was a POW and in good health. The latter statement was far from the truth but it never crossed my mind to delete it.

I couldn't remember when I last wrote to my parents but it was a long time ago. I knew that they must have been sick with worry and foreboding. With all that I had gone through it did not occur to me that the Marines would have notified them that I was missing. They would have experienced that dreaded moment for all parents with children away at war, the moment when they answered the door to find a telegraph messenger holding out the telegram. At least it would not have been the worst possible news: "Your son has been killed on active service."

I felt so guilty that I been so absorbed in my own problems that I didn't think how Mum and Dad would be suffering. They told me after the War that they received the telegram saying I was missing in July 1941 on the first day of the Glasgow Fair holiday week. A day when there was a mass exodus of Glaswegians going "Doon the Watter", as it was called, to Ayrshire holiday resorts. They were preparing to go to Largs, my favourite place on the Clyde Estuary. The only week in the year that they had a holiday was ruined. I felt so sad

The German pro-forma card to say "I am a POW". The "Good health" bit was compulsory.

1300/17/c1

I am a prisoner of war and in good health. In the next letter I will give you my address. It is useless to write before receiving the new address.

With best wishes

Name and surname: *Wm. R. Clark*

Military rank: MARINE

Designation of military formation ROYAL MARINES

for them. It must have been a dreadful blow.

Telegrams were a rarity in those days. The appearance in the street of a wee telegraph boy, wearing the conspicuous dress - blue uniform, blue hat and red bicycle - brought everything to a halt. There were eight tenements in the street, each three floors high with three houses on each floor. It was like a little village, lots of activity and chatting going on.

In wartime the appearance of the telegraph messenger had obviously a more dramatic effect. I can picture the scene, chatting in the street would stop, windows would open and all eyes would be on the telegraph messenger. A few lads were away at war. Which close would he stop at? That would tell them which house…

My Mum would be alone at the time of day. If she did know the boy was in the street, she would be struck with fear and apprehension when she opened the door and saw him with the dreaded telegram in

The telegram that all wartime parents dreaded;. "REGRET TO REPORT THAT YOUR SON CHX 100651 MARINE A R CLARK IS MISSING COMMANDANT MARINES CHATHAM"

his outstretched hand. She might have sat for ages, too petrified to open it.

Although the food at Stalag IVB was not in the category of haute cuisine, it rather felt like that to me after the recent traumatic and dramatic deprivation of all food and drink. That marvellous first shower and the delousing made me feel almost human again, unless I happened to glance in a mirror. I was still suffering from the malaria bug. I was told that it would recur but perhaps not seriously. The dysentery had cleared and, although still a bit weak, I was recovering quite well. A period of light work and some reasonable food would see me getting back to normal and ready to take on whatever the Germans could throw at me. How could I have been so naïve? I soon learned that, to the Germans, light work and POW's were never synonymous. They were going to throw the lot at me.

Lichtovitz
The Working Camp

My first impression of the Czechoslovakian countryside was good. The journey to our new abode took us through very fertile and picturesque terrain. The road followed the lovely river Elbe, bordered by a range of hills called the Schwarze Gebirgen (Black Mountains). The summer sun was warm and everything looked beautiful. Only the presence of the German guards spoiled the image. Our future home was a small house, situated in a little village called Lichtovitz on the banks of the river Elbe. The house, now an Arbeitslager, or Working Camp, was previously a Guesthouse but the accommodation was hardly in the Five Star range.

It was, however, out in the country and the only barbed wire was around the windows. The huge Stalag IVB with its massive barbed wire surrounds would have driven me crazy. I cannot remember exactly how many of us were at Lichtovitz at the beginning, perhaps about thirty.

The German in charge of the prison camp was a Feldwebel, (a Sergeant). His title, Commandant, was rather grand for a wee camp and perhaps the title went to his head because he seemed to have illusions of grandeur. He lined us up and proceeded to address us as though he was Adolf Hitler addressing the admiring crowds in the Berlin Olympic Stadium. He spoke no English and we had no German so his histrionics were a bit wasted.

An Austrian guard with some command of English stood at his side and managed to make us understand roughly what we would be doing and where we would be working. My thoughts that our very weak condition might merit a period of light work were soon shattered. Either they thought that we were malingerers or they were unconcerned whether or not we dropped down dead. The latter approach fitted our image of the Nazi ideology of disposable slave labour.

Our new career was in a quarry on the top of the Black Mountains. Our main task would be breaking stones with a sledgehammer into manageable sizes and lifting them into wagons. I did not look forward to that unless the manageable size was negotiable and the sledgehammers were in the featherweight class – fat chance of that. The village of Lichtovitz was about a mile or so from the quarry and our transport would again be "Shank's Pony", a sort of warm up for our stone breaking. Walking was going to be a problem because we had not been issued with boots and, for most of us, our army issue had put in a lot of miles.

The next stage of our introduction was a tour of our "commodious quarters", actually a single large room. One end of the room served as a dining room, lounge and recreation room and the other as a bedroom furnished with double bunk beds. You could already see the lads preparing themselves to get off the mark quickly when the time came to grab the best position.

A sack with a modicum of straw served as a mattress, with wooden planks to make sure that you did not get curvature of the spine. Other modern bedroom luxuries such as en suite facilities were not standard, not even toilets. The toilet was a wee hut at the top of the garden. Thank God my dysentery had abated.

The guard was asked: "Where do we wash!" He looked rather surprised, as though washing was an unusual habit. He pointed to a tin bath in the corner. "That will be filled with hot water each evening when you return," he said. A wee tin bath for 30 people! That lovely shower in the Stalag was going to become but a pleasant memory.

Perhaps worried that we would think that the German reputation for cleanliness was a myth, the guard went on to assure us that we would be taken weekly to the town of Aussig where we would have a hot bath in the communal baths. The German humour, or the Austrian humour (if that is different), had not yet manifested itself so nobody had the temerity to ask whether we took a weekly bath even if it was not needed.

It was all a bit crude but maybe not any worse than many homes in those days. Sharing a tin bath with 30 others was a new experience but from an early age I had been given a good grounding in hygiene using a tin bath and it stood me in good stead.

My home in a Glasgow tenement had neither bath nor hot water. We used a large tin bath on weekdays and went once a week to a local community bathhouse and laundry for a real good soak. When my brother and I were learning to swim, we walked a couple of miles to a swimming baths in Whiteinch where we had the luxury of a hot shower. Despite the logistical difficulties, my mother taught us to keep ourselves scrupulously clean.

For a lot of the lads it was all a new experience. A new experience for me was emptying the dry toilet. The emptying itself did not bother me but I was taken aback when told to dump it in the vegetable garden! The intense and gnawing hunger during the marches on Crete had made us eat almost anything. We learned that finickytiness had no place in hunger. Our hunger now was not quite the gnawing hunger of Crete but it was more than enough to make us eat our vegetables with only a passing thought of being finicky. One of my wise old Grandma's sayings was that "hunger is the best sauce!"

Work in a stone quarry was obviously going to make us even hungrier and, as we sat down to await the first meal, we hoped that we would be given solid country food to satisfy our hunger. Hope springs eternal.

The first meal was awful, mainly potatoes with watery gravy, a very small portion of meat and a piece of dark bread that was heavy and sour. After it we were still hungry. Optimistically, we hoped that the reason for the skimpy meal was they were not prepared for our arrival. I had a vision of a working man's breakfast of bacon, sausages and eggs but, alas, the breakfast did not even live up to modern continental breakfast standards of coffee, cereals and a roll.

We felt more than a little hungry as we set off to walk to the quarry for our first day of forced labour. I forgot to mention that, theoretically, this was paid work. The non-negotiable sum of one pfennig (a penny) per day for all POW's was the going rate, no matter the quality or quantity of the work. What more motivation could a man ask for? At least no one could accuse us of helping the German war effort for financial reasons.

A bright feature of the day was the summer weather, matched by the beautiful scenery, particularly the river Elbe, sparkling in the sunlight and flanked by the Schwarz Gebirgen. Despite the rumbling tummies and the presence of an armed guard to remind us of our plight, it was a beautiful sight on a lovely summer's day.

The quarry was on top of the hills. We were not fit to do any hard labour and the long walk from the camp and the steep climb up to the quarry made it worse. It would obviously be a long time before we recovered from the effect of all that we had suffered during these last terrible weeks since Canea. It seemed an eternity. Unless our physical condition improved, I was anxious of the effect on me of a hard day's work at the quarry.

First Days at the Quarry

We reached the bottom of the quarry where a long line of large empty wagons was lined up. An elderly man, balding and burned black with the sun, looked us up and down. He was obviously very unimpressed and he had every reason to reach that conclusion. We were a sight in our tatty clothes and we must have looked as we felt, absolutely knackered. If the poor bloke had been told that he was receiving a work force to boost his output, the disbelieving look on his face as he surveyed the motley collection in front of him, spoke volumes. He was the quarry foreman and he was given the obvious nickname of Old Baldy. I never found out his real name but his title was Obmann, the German word for foreman. Old Baldy was to have a big impact on our lives from that moment on.

He made a wise decision that there was no point sending this lot to the quarry face on their first day. He intuitively decided that we would find it difficult to lift even the sledgehammer, never mind to break up stones with it. Ever an optimist, I hoped that my wish for light work was about to be fulfilled.

Opposite us was a building with outside stairs leading to a door. The stair had about thirty nine steps, (shades of John Buchan) each step being about 12 inches high. The Obmann pointed firstly to a huge pile of bags of cement and then to the door at the top of the stairs. He mimed the actions of heaving the bags on to our backs, carrying them up the steps, taking them up to the door and dumping them inside. The only semblance to light work was that by miming the procedure he did not even use empty bags. If this was light work, I dreaded to think what it was going to be like at the quarry face.

He walked down the line and selected the biggest and, hopefully from his viewpoint, the strongest men to have a first go. With a tremendous struggle, they just made it. My turn eventually came. I recalled the advice given to me by the lad in the Stalag about dropping things as though it was unintentional. My efforts to lift the bag would have won an Oscar. I sank slowly to the ground. The Obmann angrily lifted the bag as though it was made of foam and plonked it on my back. I staggered to the steps, summoned all my strength and made the first step. I hoped to convey an expression of a man making a supreme effort and digging deep down for fresh sources of strength. I actually managed a few steps but I needn't have bothered acting. My legs decided that enough was enough and began to bend. The bag slid slowly down my back, went over the edge of the step and burst in a great cloud of dust.

Oh, God! How many years would it take repaying that lot at a pfennig a day? If the Obmann had ever seen a Hollywood film he might, like the New York Mafia, have stuck my feet in a wet bag of cement and dropped me in the river Elbe. Fortunately the Austrian guard had a sense of humour and, trying not to laugh, said something to the Obmann. Old Baldy had so far not revealed an addiction to laughter and he turned away in disgust so my life was spared.

Although this incident was brought about by my weakness and not by my acting, the technique worked so I kept it in mind for another suitable occasion. The art of faking was against my nature but I was determined to do as little as possible for the Germans without getting into trouble. I hoped that my performance would earn me a spell of light work. Although it was obvious that the Obmann considered lifting cement bags was relatively light work, he must have decided that he had not enough cement bags to persevere with me as a cement bag lifter. He then led me to what I hoped would be a job more suited to my puny muscles.

He stopped at an Everest-looking mountain of stone chips, handed me an enormous fork and indicated that I should use it to load stones into a wagon. Could he possibly believe that this was light work? I quickly realised that lifting that fork full of stones would have me knackered in no time so I decided to load it with as few stones as possible.

Once more my scheming proved unnecessary because on my first effort the stones dribbled through the tines of the fork. "What a stupid implement," I thought: "What on earth was wrong with a shovel?" The Obmann was keeping his beady eye on me. After my cement bag-lifting debacle, my pitiful efforts to get any stones at all on the damned thing drove him crazy. Grabbing the fork from me he pointed to the ends of the prongs, which, unlike forks of my experience, were flattened. He then pushed it deep into the mound and lifted an enormous amount of stones without one stone slipping through. The wagon shuddered with the impact as he hurtled them in. After this demonstration I continued, blandly, to lose most of my load.

Teams of two were allocated to each wagon. The Obmann noted the prowess with the fork of one Cecil Bareham, a lad from a farm in Blo Norton, a village in Norfolk. He was quite used to working with a fork and his muscles were still like steel rods. He had an effortless way of using the fork and looked as though he could go on all day without a break. He pushed the fork into the heap of stones and with the smooth swing of a professional golfer, landed them in the wagon without dropping even a wee stone. He loaded a wagon in no time.

Consequently and to Cecil's embarrassment, the Obmann decided with a stroke of management acumen to team me with Cecil. Either he expected that I would eventually emulate Cecil's efforts or that Cecil would add enough extra stones to make up for my deficiency. I had no intention of imitating Cecil's workload even if I could.

Considering Old Baldy's opinion of me, Cecil was highly embarrassed when it became immediately obvious that he was the Obmann's model and favourite. When the Obmann departed in disgust, Cecil revealed some of the secrets of using a fork to load stones successfully. The fork was designed with flat ends so that it slid under the stones instead of digging into them. A big load on the fork prevented the stones slipping through. I thanked Cecil but pointed out that at present I had no wish to attain that success. Apart from the fact that I would soon be knackered lifting a big load, I was still trying to learn how to do as little as possible without being found out.

The "stone breakers" back from quarry still wearing pre-1941 clothes.
Above left, the Author (on left) and Cecil.

So far I had managed to do as little as possible but I had still to learn the knack of not being found out. It was a habit of a lifetime for Cecil to work at a certain pace so his big loads and my wee ones made an average good load. Not a bad start to what turned out to a great friendship.

A small churn was sent out from Lichtovitz and awaited us at the midday break. If we expected that the food would be substantial, we were soon disappointed. The soup was so thin that it looked as if the cook had just dipped the vegetables into hot water to make it smell like soup. Closer examination revealed that there was actually vegetable sediment at the bottom so we decided that it must be soup. It was duly dished out and there was no main course, not a meal by any standard suitable for hard labour.

The end of that first day could not come quickly enough. The tribulations of the past events had taken its toll and Old Baldy was driving us very hard. He would consider my performance as abysmal and probably thought it was deliberate. While I had no intention of working my guts out for Germany maybe they had some right to expect a reasonable return for food and keep.

My output on my first day's work might only have merited the small midday meal but a normal day's work at the quarry face needed a lot more than that. The Obmann was not too bright and probably did not appreciate what we had been through so the next few weeks at least were going to be difficult. He might, I suspect, have felt that the British are all born lazy and idle.

The long walk back to Lichtovitz for some of us was a wee bit reminiscent of the Via Dolorosa in so far as we were awfie tired, had sore feet and aching muscles. On the other hand there was great speculation about the forthcoming meal. We hoped that the lunchtime soup was not an indicator of the quality and quantity of the dinner.

A very weary group trailed into the camp. The tin bath of hot water was sufficient only to soak swollen feet and chapped hands for those who had been working at the quarry face. When the main meal arrived, it was again a real disappointment. It was a repeat of the previous day's dinner, a handful of potatoes in their skins, the same watery gravy, a small piece of meat from an unidentifiable animal and a piece of the black bread that smelled and tasted sour.

It turned out that the texture of the bread was normal here and was rated quite highly by the locals. Black bread, unlike fresh bread as we knew it, made you feel full and it took a long time to go mouldy. We protested that nobody could do heavy work on that diet. The answer was that the Czechs, and indeed the Germans, were all on strict rations and that we were no worse off than the civilians. The military were on special rations but obviously military was no longer our classification.

Enquiries next day from the Czechs working in the quarry confirmed that this was indeed true because Czech families were in a very bad way. An indication that rations were low was a warning that it was forbidden to peel potatoes unless you ate the peelings. It looked as though we were going to be permanently on near starvation rations, a poor outlook indeed. Spirits were low that night and most of us made straight for bed. Exhaustion led quickly to sleep and sleep gave a respite for a few hours from the misery.

The warning about potato peelings reminds me that there was a fair cross section of the social classes even in such a small sample of Brits as that at Lichtovitz. High standards of table manners were not something that was expected of you in our circumstances. Indeed hunger and small rations created a tendency to wolf it all down in no time flat. However, Eric Judd, a banker in Civvy Street (civilian life) with whom I struck up a good friendship, created an amusing incident.

Some of the lads, whose table manners were not up to Savoy standards, found it hilarious. Very early in our arrival at Lichtovitz we were warned that strict rationing meant that any wastage of food was verboten (forbidden) and was a punishable offence. Verboten was used so often that it became our best known German word.

As the first tatties were dished up the warning about disposing of the peelings anywhere but in your belly was emphasised. Most of us were so very hungry that we needed no warning. But as yet, hunger had not yet made Eric relinquish a lifetime of culinary habits. Not wishing to be seen eating potato peelings, he leaned across the table to me and said very politely: "I say, Alex, would you care for my potato peelings?"

He kept such a dead straight face that for a moment there was no reaction to his kind gesture. I expressed my thanks and responded in kind by eating the peelings with due decorum as if it were caviar. Eric's action was a good reminder to us to try to keep some standards. He certainly did that. Although he looked nothing like a banker in his present garb, I could imagine Eric in his bowler hat, pin stripes, spats and umbrella walking into the bank. I could just picture him lifting his bowler to me as he handed over the peelings.

Eric had a real sense of humour. When he delivered a riposte he kept a straight face, sometimes betrayed by a glint in his eyes. His responses were not always in the image of his banker profession. A lovely example of that was his riposte to a remark made that the handling of the Battle of Crete was a load of shit. "In that case," said Eric, "if that is so, it would be apposite that all of us who were involved in the Battle of Crete should be known as Excretians."

The next morning, I was sent to the quarry face to work with a tall and strong looking Czech whose name was Jan. The Obmann spoke to the Czech and pointed to me. I was sure that he would be telling him that he would have to look out for me because I was idle, lazy and accident-prone. I was handed a whacking big sledgehammer that weighed a ton. At least it felt like a ton but it actually weighed about 8lbs. The quarry face had been recently blasted so there was a mass of huge stones waiting to be broken up and loaded onto the wagon. The Obmann held up his hand, pointed to the pile of stones, made a gesture of breaking them up, pointed to the wagon and lifted ten fingers. Presumably that was the number of wagons that I was supposed to fill. Either he had a hitherto undisclosed sense of humour or he was thick between the ears. Ten stones, maybe, but not ten wagons. Obviously a confrontation was in the air.

I lifted the sledgehammer above my head. Even that was an effort for me. I selected a smallish stone and gave it a whack, making my whole body shudder. I felt like Tom in the "Tom and Jerry" cartoons, when Tom breaks into little pieces after Jerry, the wee Mouse, gives him a real clout. My first lesson in breaking stones had begun.

Jan firstly said that normally a stone that size did not need to be broken up and should be lifted directly into the wagon. He then chose a monstrous stone and pointed out a vein running across it. He told me to hit the stone along that vein line and it should crack quite easily. Aware that my wallop would probably not crack the stone as easily as Jan anticipated, I gave it my best bash. Lo and behold, to my utter astonishment, the stone cracked. I stood back and admired my handiwork.

That provoked a strong reaction from the Obmann. With his low opinion of me as a potential quarryman, he probably thought that I looked on cracking one huge stone as a satisfactory day's work, that I hadn't twigged that you were expected to load the stones into the wagon and to keep on loading all day. But he hadn't twigged that I was practising doing as little as possible. With the help of Jan, who frequently slipped a few stones into my wagon when the Obmann was not looking, I managed to load a couple of wagons by the end of the day. It was miles below the minimum but nobody said anything. My hands and arms were nearly falling off but at least I was still standing upright by the end of the day. I hadn't done my quota but neither had any of the other POW's.

The tin bath arrangement for washing was, as you would expect, so unsatisfactory that by the end of a week we were all very much in need of a bath. The trip to Aussig was always eagerly awaited. The eagerness was dimmed a wee bit because the transport was by "Shank's Pony". Some of us had been issued with clogs to replace our worn out boots.

Walking in clogs is a technique that we had not yet mastered. The local Czechs, especially the kids, could run about all over the place in clogs but we were still at the slithery stage.

Our clothes were anything but smart and attracted a lot of attention as we entered Aussig. No doubt the Czechs thought that, if we represented the Allied Army, the prospects of defeating the Third Reich were slim. We smiled and waved to people as we passed and got an amiable response. The guard put a stop to that and the effect on the locals was immediate. They melted away. Obviously the Germans ruled the occupied territories with a rod of iron and we learned fast that any fraternising with the Czechs could have disastrous consequences for them.

Our clothes still made us look a ragged lot but we came out of the baths feeling like a million dollars. That walk each week became a highlight in our lives.

The food at the lunch break did not improve and it was obviously not going to improve. We were fast approaching the bad weather of winter. We had already protested about the rations but we were growing more desperate, so, again I raised the matter with the Commandant. He did not blow his top but he repeated the previous reply that we received the same as the Czechs.

One lunch break, before we dished out the soup, someone made a suggestion. Instead of everyone getting a watery serving of soup every day, we should not stir the soup. The sediment at the bottom would make a reasonable dish for a few. A rota could be made and we would all enjoy our soup at least once in a while. To my astonishment the suggestion was unanimously accepted which I thought was marvellous, especially with not a Union official within hundreds of miles. Perhaps that was why we reached agreement so easily. When a few people are confined in close proximity day after day, there were bound to be difficulties in "relations" (a euphemistic phrase for a punch up) so reaching an agreement by consensus was a good omen.

The Commandant said that we had to appoint a Vertrauensmann.

The Austrian said that this meant a "trusted man". In view of the efforts to persuade us to co-operate, we immediately reacted adversely, thinking that it meant trusted by the Germans. We accepted the proposal when it was explained that a Vertrauensmann was a person whom the prisoners would accept to speak and act on their behalf.

After a discussion I was asked to take on the duty. I was hesitant because I spoke absolutely no German and I was also reluctant to cross swords with the Commandant who was a rabid Nazi. I decided to accept the task on the understanding that the Austrian guard who had a smattering of English might help me. That plan faltered, like many of my plans during these last few months, because he left shortly afterwards. I had no books to help me and I had already experienced the cock-ups you could make using body language.

The Nazi stance and lack of a sense of humour so far displayed by the Commandant was a potentially lethal combination. I might have been in trouble if, say, a request made by hand actions for toilet rolls and was interpreted that he was a shit. My first efforts as a translator using body language were often misinterpreted and many very awkward and sometimes very farcical moments arose.

An example was a discussion on the lack of fresh items in our diet. On the subject of fresh eggs, the appropriate body action was to squat and flap my arms but the Commandant was obviously not sure what I meant. Perhaps he thought that I had diarrhoea.

A new guard arrived who made me think about typecasting individuals according to their nationality. Before the War, the aggressive and cruel Prussian aristocrat with cold blue eyes was my image of a typical German. In POW camps, that image still applied. Perhaps a surfeit of Hollywood films contributed to that conception, though some of the SS troops we encountered more than fitted the bill.

In reality people are firstly individuals with different characteristics despite the tendency for environment and upbringing in different cultures to standardise them. Look how we joke about the mean Scots, not to mention the dim Irish and the superiority of the English.

Thus, whereas the Commandant, the Obmann and the Quarry manager conformed to our stereotyped impression of a German and a Nazi, the new guard completely upset that conception. He was elderly; anyone over thirty was elderly when you were twenty. He spoke quietly and he was a soft, gentle, kindly, and inoffensive man who wouldn't hurt a fly. He carried his rifle like a walking stick and walked with a long and slow stride.

He was probably called up to the forces because of his age and the need to release younger men for the Eastern Front. We immediately dubbed him the Gent. When he was on duty the atmosphere was much more relaxed. I realised that life in Nazi Germany must have been very difficult for many people of his disposition. I could not see the Gent accepting any of the Nazi culture but, like most Germans, he dare not whisper such views even within his family because any expression of disapproval with the Nazi regime had long ago been stifled.

I wrote earlier about my impressions of the large Stalag IVB. I preferred the working camp because at least you were out in the open air, although I realised how much I was missing the intellectual activities of the life I had lived, seemingly so long ago now. I don't mean anything profound but some of the activities I missed would be available in the larger Stalags – libraries, discussion groups, drama groups, music, and film shows.

Our camp had no access to these things. In any case the long hours of heavy work and the lack of nutritious food meant that your energy, mental and physical, was completely sapped. Most of us were so tired and hungry and weak when we arrived back from work that we went straight to bed after the meal. We hadn't much time for the niceties of life.

There were, however, some advantages of living in a small camp. You got to know everyone well in a short time and that made it easier to help one another in the very difficult circumstances of a life so strange to us. We did not have the ever-threatening barbed wire fences that surrounded the perimeter of Stalags, a constant reminder of our incarceration. Going out to work perhaps only extended the boundaries of our prison. The freedom that we previously took so much for granted was no longer ours, we still had the guard with his gun to remind us of that.

As time passed I became more and more aware that one of the disadvantages of living in a small working camp was the build up of tension caused by so few people living in close proximity. People's habits, social and physical, are not so irritating if you meet them infrequently. The same habits could drive you daft when you heard or observed them day after day, night after night, week after week, month after month and even year after year. We had no leisure activities and conversation began to get threadbare. In one large room there was no place where you could be alone and you felt like a goldfish in a bowl. I often longed for a good book that would give me mental privacy.

No period was easy for a POW in Germany but this particular period, 1941, was very difficult. The star of the German Army was in its ascendancy. Their forces had met no resistance in Czechoslovakia. The Luftwaffe had devastated Warsaw before the Wehrmacht conquered Poland. They had had a fantastic success against the Allied forces with the fall of Holland, Belgium, France, and the withdrawal of the British forces, culminating in the evacuation at Dunkirk and finally the debacle of Greece and Crete.

The Germans felt the world was at Adolf Hitler's feet. Those in control of POW's were cock-a-hoop. The Germans declared war on the Russians at about this time and that was the reason why they were in such a desperate hurry to get us away from Crete and on to Germany. Hitler wanted as many troops as possible for the attack on Russia.

Now the Germans were boasting that even the mighty Russia would soon fall and Germany would then have all of Europe under its control. Their constant theme was that our destiny was in their hands and that those who co-operated and worked hard for the Reich would be treated favourably. They might even be given trusted work in occupied countries.

If we did not co-operate, well, that was the hidden threat. In front of the Germans, we always tried to keep a brave face and not to appear despondent or pessimistic. It was not easy when black clouds hid the horizon of the future and POW existence might go on ad infinitum. We sang songs and whistled as we marched to the quarry. Probably we were whistling in the wind but, just as on the march to Sphakia, it kept our spirits up and showed the Germans that we were unimpressed with their boasting.

News from Home

The event of the year, my first letter from home, helped to blow away the doldrums, at least for a wee while. Although the letter was newsy and short, I devoured it (not literally!) again and again. The contents of the letter were a real breath from home and I have to confess that I was close to tears of nostalgia and homesickness. I felt so far from home.

Adhering to my philosophy of coping with the present by projecting my thoughts to a future of freedom was becoming increasingly difficult. I read the letter repeatedly, but it was not just my Mum's words of love that stirred my feelings. It was the memories it evoked of home. As I read it, I was transported back walking down the street, chatting to family and friends. I was free as a bird, going on weekend trips "Doon the Watter", crossing on the ferry from Gourock to Dunoon and cycling back by the Cowal Peninsula to Glasgow.

I treasured that letter for its evocation of these lovely, nostalgic journeys, but with it also came another treasure, a real treasure, a literary treasure. My Mum sent me a book called Palgraves Golden Treasury. She could not have made a wiser choice if she herself had been a POW for years. It was an old school book containing a selection of the poems of some the most renowned poets down the years. It was like manna from heaven.

When I was at school, Palgraves Golden Treasury was the bane of my life. I was not too keen on poetry at that age, mainly because I was forced to learn by heart so many poems that I did not like. I was forever forgetting to swot up a poem out of the Treasury that I had been given for homework. At that time I would have ridiculed anyone who described that book as manna from heaven. Yet now it was such a joy, a real golden treasure.

There were so many wisecracks from lads who thought that reading poetry was only for softies that I desperately wanted to find a quiet corner to read my book. There were no quiet corners in a crowded one-room establishment so I went to my bed, curled up and read until my eyelids refused to stay open. When I awoke in the morning the wee square of barbed wire around the window brought me back to reality with a bang. Oh! The pangs of homesickness were so overpowering. Even as I write about it now, after almost 60 years, strong emotions still surface.

Life at the Quarry

Our morale and physical condition were perhaps at their worst in the period from autumn until the end of the year 1941. The food remained at a level insufficient to sustain us for work in the quarry. Clothes and boots were wearing thin and the weather was getting colder.

On the war front, the Germans were claiming to have advanced well into Russia and they forecast that Moscow would fall to them by the end of the year. Their claim was probably not accurate but we had no wireless nor access to reliable news from Britain to confirm or deny the report. Our guards kept us informed of the outpourings from the Propaganda Minister, Herr Goebbels, who was renowned for releasing good news only.

I hoped that Hitler had bitten off more than he could chew when he tackled the mighty Russia but if the Russian army had been pushed back to the Capital, Hitler might possibly be on the verge of conquering the whole of Europe. I hated to admit it, even to myself, but that possibility might soon be a probability. Our future prospects were dim and I wondered whether I would ever see home again.

The Germans were ruthless in their use of the population of occupied countries. I didn't want to allow such negative thoughts to dominate my thinking so I recalled that Napoleon had also considered himself invincible. He too pushed hard in his effort to take Moscow before winter set in but the fierce Russian winter proved to be his downfall. Maybe Hitler would suffer the same fate. I clung to that positive thought.

But winter was also making itself felt in Czechoslovakia and it brought real hardships. The Germans asserted that they expected the Red Cross to supply us with military clothing and boots. We had heard about the marvellous Red Cross food parcels sent from home but as yet there was no sign of either food or clothing.

The temperature in Sudetenland often dropped well below freezing. When the snow turned to ice, the main road to Praskovitz became a nightmare. The climb up the steep hill to the quarry was even worse, particularly for the few with clogs, the leather uppers and wooden soled variety.

I had no previous knowledge of clogs but my opinion of them as winter footwear soon leapt up enormously. Undoubtedly they were treacherous on the ice but brown paper wrapped around your feet provided first-rate insulation (except when the paper got wet and then froze). Those who had boots that had worn thin and with gloves made up from bits of cloth, suffered from frost bitten toes and hands. This applied particularly to those working at the quarry face.

Split hands and festering sores were normal in ordinary temperatures but if you had no gloves when the temperature dropped to well below zero, a careless grip of the sides of a wagon could result in your hand sticking firmly to the metal. A hasty effort to release your hand could leave flesh still sticking to the wagon. I had developed a split in the palm of my hand and the cold was aggravating it.

I asked Anton how he coped with that problem. He showed me the palm of his hands. Over a long period, the impact of sledgehammer on stone had worn a permanent hole in the palm of his hands where he gripped the sledgehammer. It had festered at first but over the years it had formed a hard skin. I shuddered at the prospect of developing a sore like that. He hesitated before telling me a good way to harden the skin – urinate on it!

Mentioning the icy weather reminds me of an incident concerning the hut that served as our toilet. It amused everyone, except the participants. You would not expect a well-appointed toilet at the top of a quarry. It wasn't. A hut without a door, a plank fixed between the walls with a space behind it and a hole in the ground served the purpose.

You can't call a hole in the ground by a civilised name such as lavatory, loo or toilet. A bog was the accepted word. It sounds like a hole in the ground, so I shall call it the bog.

The bog was functional and, providing you had absolutely no sense of smell, it was acceptable. In hot weather and in high winds, there was no doubt where the bog was. Frequently a new hole had to be dug and, although I preferred light work, I avoided the bog duty whenever possible.

In anticipation of the heavy frosts with the approach of winter, a number of holes were dug in advance of winter because of the difficulty of digging a hole in an ice bound surface. A few of the lads who were not considered robust enough to work at the quarry-face were on permanent light work. Shifting the bog was one of their responsibilities.

The hut had slots for two long poles for lifting and walking it to the new site. During a very icy spell the hut had to be moved. The hut was quite heavy so their progress was slow and rather sedate, rather like the aristocrats being carried in their sedan chairs in days gone by. We usually whistled a slow march to keep in time with their measured steps. To co-ordinate the start, the one in front shouted "One, two, three and Hup," and then "Forward" and they lifted the hut together. The one at the back (I shall not name him) was not paying attention. As a result he landed in the bog but fortunately for him the contents of the bog were frozen hard. There was still a real pong clinging to him and when we left for the camp the guard kept him well to the windward.

In winter the walk back down the hill from the quarry in freezing conditions was made even more difficult by a combination of weary limbs and clogs. I don't recall anyone being seriously injured. On several occasions I actually enjoyed that winter descent even although it destroyed any dignity to which POW's might lay claim. These circumstances only arose during the school winter holidays. It would have been good material for the old-fashioned black and white Hollywood slapstick comedies.

The Praskovitz kids were experts on skis. The arrival of British POW's introduced a new and engrossing element to their skiing. They went to the top of the hill above the quarry and waited out of sight for us to come down the hill at the end of our day's work. Choosing their moment with fiendish accuracy, when we were slithering down at the steepest part of the gradient, they came over the top howling like Sioux Indians on the warpath. Descending on us in force, they zigzagged across the hill at high speed. Although they didn't deliberately knock anyone over, some of us over-balanced as they skilfully manoeuvred in and out as though we were markers on a slalom course. The winner was probably the one who caused most POW's to stumble. It showed that kids are kids the world over until they grow up and are indoctrinated by adult prejudices, racist and otherwise.

At home in Britain, the diet in winter usually switched from salads to hot thick soups and substantial portions of meat and veg. At

Praskovitz, by contrast, as the months passed into the winter of 1941, the only changes in the diet were that the soup became thinner and thinner and the rations became tighter and tighter.

Almost a Strike

Time passed and the inadequate food was becoming a real problem. We hadn't had a decent meal since before the march in Crete and now we were faced with work heavier than most of us had ever experienced, certainly in these conditions. My arms had developed quite a bit with using the sledgehammer but I was beginning to feel constantly tired. I was not surprised when my ribs began to stick out. What surprised me was that, although we were skinny, a number of us had developed fairly big stomachs. One of the lads who had been stationed in Africa said some of the natives were skin and bone but yet had huge stomachs. They were suffering from malnutrition.

That had us all thinking hard. There was no doubt that I had been undernourished since Crete but I didn't know how long and to what degree one had to be undernourished before it was classed as starvation or malnutrition. The chance of an increase in quality and quantity of our food seemed most unlikely because of the severe rationing in Germany. My approach was the same as with all my problems during this period of my life. If you cannot do anything about a problem, there was no point in worrying about it. Hopefully the swollen stomach was caused by wind.

Other lads were not so philosophical. Winter was upon us. Our Army clothes and boots were well worn. Those who did not even have socks had packed their boots with paper to keep out the cold. We set out one day when the weather was bad and the conditions made the long walk and climb up to the quarry more strength-sapping than usual. It was one of those wet wintry days when a high wind was driving into your face and your clothes became heavy with the rain. The ground at the quarry face was wet and soggy. With leaking boots and gloves made up from odd pieces of cloth, we had cold hands and wet feet and were thoroughly miserable.

The work was no harder than usual but it was inevitable that the cumulative affect of hunger and working day after day in very difficult conditions would build up a reaction. Add to all that the effect of the infamous barbed wire madness and it was odds on that a fuse was bound to blow. After an accumulation of aggravations it is often a very insignificant thing that causes a fuse to blow.

When the midday break came, the soup was even thinner than usual and the sediment served was less than normal. The thinner soup was the last straw that broke the camel's back and a number of the lads wanted to take some action.

A small group of POW's in an isolated country working camp has not an awful lot of clout so we were hardly in a position to do very much. I had some experience of representing staff in a Civil Service Union but I had no illusions about the status of trade unionists in Nazi Germany. I had no enthusiasm about being the sole representative of the first and probably the last Praskovitz POW Union of Quarry Workers!

The majority supported my view that a strike affecting our output would be suicidal. Instead we would plead that lack of food and inadequate clothing in this inclement weather had made us all too weak to work any more that day. I expected that, as their Vertrauensmann, I should present their case. I was sure that a declaration of intention to stop work in Nazi Germany was not part of my remit but I was in a minority of one. I was not at all keen on that task and, with my strong sense of survival there was no way that I would risk the firing squad for an issue as feeble as thin soup.

My limited German would be hopelessly inadequate to convey to the guard that, although we intended to stop work, he must not interpret it as the long-established British custom of striking. I was doubtful whether the SS would become involved in such a minor issue but their main negotiation weapon would probably have bullets in it.

The guard that day was the Gent and at first he just smiled when I told him that we could not carry on working. He obviously thought that he did not understand my German. Often he just smiled when he didn't understand me. When it dawned on him that Prisoners of War were actually refusing to work because of thin soup, he looked at me in disbelief. He would be thinking that this did not happen in the Third Reich. I was sorry for him because he would get some big stick for not sorting it out.

When we did not respond to his demand that we return to work, he called for the Obmann to take over. The Gent disappeared, presumably to contact his superiors.

I was apprehensive that the first question he would be asked when he contacted them might be "Have you shot them?" I also had an uneasy feeling that he would be told to warn us to go back to work immediately and to reinforce the order by pointing his rifle at me. Long before he returned, I rehearsed my speech of capitulation, also my resignation as Vertrauensmann with immediate effect. The guard re-appeared accompanied by a Feldwebel and it might have been just a co-incidence that he had the expressionless and cold eyes that one associates with the SS. My eyes, on the other hand, were full of expression and were fixed firmly on the customary pistol at his side.

The gent pointed to me and said: "Vertrauensmann". I hoped that I would be given a chance to speak before he fired. He looked at me and then at the alleged rebels and he obviously doubted that such a decrepit lot were a serious threat to the Third Reich. He then looked in the churn of soup, shook his head and spoke to the Guard. Although he spoke quickly I understood some of the words, 'Schlecht' (bad), 'Sprechen' (speak), 'Frau' (woman) and 'Kuchin' (cook). It sounded hopeful and I was delighted that he was not the ogre that I first thought.

I did not hear him use the word 'Schiesen' (shoot), but he touched his holster as if to show that he was not to be trifled with. He pointed firstly to us, then waved to the quarry face, saying: "Schnell" (fast). I gave the lads an ad hoc and a very loose interpretation. It was to the effect that he agreed that the soup was far too thin and that he would see that the cook was told to improve it immediately but only if we returned to work at once.

It wasn't quite along the lines of my capitulation speech but it served the same purpose. Some of the lads who had a few words of German knew that I was chancing my arm. The others might have thought that it took a helluva lot of English words to interpret a few German words. Actually, I was surprised at his mild reaction but that did not stop my knees from knocking. It might have been different if I had been daft enough to protest but for me the "Mini-strike that never was" had ended. There is a time and place for standing firm but this wasn't the time, Nazi Germany wasn't the place and thin soup was definitely not worth the ultimate punishment. My brief career as a negotiator was over.

I didn't notice much difference in the soup next day so my interpretation could have been inaccurate – my, my, how surprising! I wondered whether we were the first British POW's to consider a strike in Nazi Germany and had made a bit of history. Could my brief encounter with the strikebusting Feldwebel have qualified as one of the "Almost a Hero" occasions? I think not. Anyone who gave his life for thin soup would have been certified as non compos mentis rather than heroic.

Injuries in the Quarry

The winter conditions saw a spate of injuries. In addition to those caused by inadequate apparel and unsafe equipment, many other injuries were commonplace for those working at the quarry face. One cause was moving the stones by hand into a position whereby they could be broken. Sometimes two large stones would slip, come together and crush your hands.

On one occasion a serious injury to a POW (I cannot recall his name but I'll call him John) resulted in the severance of a finger. Fortunately he showed tremendous presence of mind and instead of panicking, he picked up his finger, stuck it onto the stump and yelled for someone to get him to hospital. I was impressed that the Obmann showed concern for all his workers in matters like these, even for POW's.

The lad was down the mountain in no time and off to the hospital. I was puzzled as to why John should be so determined to keep the severed part jammed against stump, unless it was to stem the flow of blood. If his injury was attended to in time, it might be some consolation to him if he were not sent back to work in the quarry. But to my astonishment he returned in a relatively short time.

I expected to see a space where his missing finger used to be. There was a bandage but no space. I thought, surely you can't get a dummy finger and why would a dummy finger need a bandage? He thoroughly enjoyed my consternation and waggled his finger. It wasn't a dummy, it was his own finger! The German surgeons had made tremendous strides in surgery because they had to cope with so many war casualties. Nowadays when so many of parts of the body can be replaced with transplants, sewing on a finger would not excite any attention. In 1941, it seemed a miracle to me because I did not know that it was possible to keep a severed member and have it sown on afterwards.

Weakness and very cold conditions were no doubt partly to blame for increased injuries. In these conditions accidents were bound to happen because both our hands and the stones were cold and wet. Having no gloves didn't help. Heavy, slippery sledgehammers could fly off at a tangent when you tried to break a large stone. In frosty conditions the palms of your hands and the fingers could crack open. I had to go to hospital on three occasions with such injuries. The jarring effect of hitting stones with a sledgehammer over a period of time caused a considerable swelling across the palm of my hands, just below the fingers.

The doctor said that, because of its scarcity, anaesthetic was only used for serious cases and my case was not considered serious. He picked up a knife, held my hand open and proceeded to cut the swellings. I had to hold a pad to my hand until the flow of blood was stemmed. The wound was bandaged and that was the end of the treatment.

I got similar "bite the bullet" treatment later when my thumbnail had to be removed because my thumb was crushed and badly damaged by a large stone. The doctor took out a pair of forceps, held my hand tight and whipped the nail off. This time I gave a loud yell because I had neither any anaesthetic nor a bullet to bite! I don't mean to give the impression that German doctors were deliberately cruel. They were obviously disturbed that they had not enough anaesthetics and I understood that scarce supplies should be reserved for the severely injured soldiers.

I wrote earlier about the POW in the Stalag who initiated me into ways of avoiding work without being punished. He deliberately dropped bags so that the contents spilled out, but he made it look as if was a clumsy accident. While I was waiting to have my thumb dressed, I met a real character, a POW who had made a fine art in avoiding work. He told me that he had hardly ever worked since he became a POW. I listened carefully - all ears - hoping I would not be called away before he revealed his masterly secret.

It was simple. He complained of severe pains in the area around his abdomen and when he was told to get ready to go to hospital, he rolled silver paper into little balls and swallowed them. On the x-ray machine they showed up as dark patches. He had been getting treatment for it ever since. He added some more silver paper each time he went into hospital. I was called away before I could ask him how he stopped the silver paper passing through him.

He said that another guise for avoiding work was to rub your skin with a knife until it bled. With luck, it would be diagnosed as a chronic ulcer and you repeated the process when the wound healed. I thought that there must be a less painful way of avoiding work. It was a case of the cure being a damn sight worse than the symptom. As he didn't claim that this was his way of sabotaging the German war effort, I suspected that avoiding work was a way of life for him. If his idea caught on in prison camps there would be a big run on silver paper. He seemed surprised that my injury was actually unintentional.

Red Cross Parcels

The arrival of Red Cross Parcels was one of the biggest events in prison camp life. This was especially so in 1941 and early 1942 in Lichtovitz and Prascovitz, when we were almost at the point of starvation. The parcels were like manna from heaven and they provided not only a big improvement to our diet but also those little luxuries, such as chocolate, that we took for granted at home.

Their beneficial effect went much wider than these material things. Letters from home, despite their infrequency were much needed and helped to dispel the depression that "barbed wire madness" provokes. Red Cross parcels were a contact with home and made us feel not only that our family remembered us, but that other people who did not know us were aware of our plight and wanted to help. That was greatly appreciated. Some parcels had a card inserted with a note of the name and address of the sponsors. I was delighted that, after the war, I was able personally to express my gratitude to a group who sponsored one of my parcels. That lovely and pleasant experience is recounted in Appendix D.

The distribution of Red Cross parcels was entirely in the hands of the Germans and, considering the very stringent rationing in Germany and the marvellous contents of the parcels, those involved in their distribution must have felt a tremendous temptation to pilfer. Although I cannot remember exactly when the parcels arrived, I still recall the excitement when we were told that a consignment was expected. I recall even more vividly the joyous scene when the

Author & Cecil

Jock from Dundee

The band – few instruments – nearly all singers

Entire camp in new uniforms

The workers

Barbed wire madness? No, just plain daft.

moment arrived to open them. It had been so long since we had seen "luxuries", such as commonplace items like corned beef had now become.

I cannot recall any serious cases of stealing ever being reported and that really did impress me. There was one "incident", but whether it was actually a theft or just a practical joke that went wrong (and the perpetrator was too frightened to own up) was never revealed.

Bill was a "hoarder" and he had a real yen for a freshly baked loaf, not the black and sour kind we usually got. A Czech worker agreed to bring such a loaf - that was the easy part of the deal. But when Bill obtained it, he was faced with a difficult problem, avoiding detection at the search when entering the camp. It was a long loaf and hiding something that length was not so easy. The success or otherwise of avoiding detection depended on which guard was on duty on the day.

There was seldom a search when leaving the quarry. Pushing a long shaped loaf down a trouser leg was the favourite technique but a problem with that method was practising to walk normally. At first a limp was used to disguise the effect of the loaf on the walk but that ruse was soon rumbled. Another disadvantage of the leg method was that the atmosphere down the leg was apt to pollute the lovely aroma of a freshly baked loaf, ruining one of its big attractions.

Another method was to stuff it up the back of a jacket. At least that method made you erect and you walked like a Marine on the parade ground. The detection rate of something with a smell, such as a loaf, is decreased if the guard has a heavy cold. Otherwise a bit of luck helps and Bill was lucky. The search was cursory so Bill had a nice fresh slice of white bread with his meal. He took the remainder of the loaf to bed that night and placed it under his pillow for safety. He must have slept like a log because he gave a yell in the morning that would have awakened the dead.

His loaf was gone. The thief must either have had a sensitive touch like a pickpocket or he waited until Bill turned in his sleep. The loaf was never found, a feat that seemed impossible in such a confined area. If the thief ate it all, he must have had a real sore stomach and been dead worried about passing wind all night and giving the show away. A theft is a theft but I couldn't help having a sneaking admiration for the audacity of it. The mystery of the disposal of the loaf was never solved.

The influence of the Red Cross parcels on our health and on our morale was tremendous. I could tell many stories about that. However, before I decided to write this book I wrote a short story based on the parcels. It was about a POW who gave a fellow Czech worker a bar of chocolate, intended as a rare luxury for his young daughter. The Czech offered a couple of eggs to show his appreciation.

The main purpose of writing the story was to convey some idea of one aspect of life in a POW camp. It was well received and was published. Although fiction, it was based on an actual incident. (I have inserted it in Appendix B and hope that the reader will enjoy it).

The year 1941, one of the worst years in my life, was dragging itself to a conclusion. Although rations were still very poor, the Red Cross parcels continued to boost our morale. They had improved our lives but they were really only meant as a supplement and were not a daily feature.

Working at the quarry on these rations in winter conditions was still taking its toll. As 1941 drew to its close, thoughts of Hogmanay and all the festivities that we enjoyed back home in Scotland came to mind. At home, bringing in the New Year was an enjoyable tradition that brought families together and was always well celebrated. Resolutions for the incoming year were readily and optimistically made and just as readily broken.

Obviously there was not much cause to celebrate Hogmanay in 1941. We looked back over the departing year, resolved to try to learn from mistakes we'd made and to take heart from our successes.

I sat on my bed, dwelling nostalgically on past Hogmanays and looking back over the worst year in my life. There was nothing to be gained by dwelling too long on that terrible year, on situations present and even less cause to dwell on the future. Despite the awful circumstances of the present, I felt that I should count myself lucky to be alive and reasonably fit and well. I cannot remember making a specific resolution, but I do remember deciding to stick to the thought that had sustained me in Crete and ever since. The present is only a blip in time and although it might be full of trouble, strife and depression, it will pass as all things pass. Lift your head up and focus your eyes on the future when better times will inevitably come.

Praskovitz

In 1942 our numbers increased to about fifty and we moved to a new location in the neighbouring village of Praskovitz. It was another former Guest House that had been converted to serve as a POW camp. Apart from internal alterations, the main change was the erection of barbed wire on top of a wall. A thoughtful gesture just to make us feel at home!

Actually the need for the barbed wire was that we had access to the garden so it was quite an improvement. The building also had much roomier accommodation. The village of Praskovitz was on the banks of the Elbe and, as the quarry was on the hill above the village, we did not have the long walk every day. The Guest House had a kitchen that was available to us as part of our quarters.

A cook came in daily and, despite the poor quality and quantity of food available to her, she tried to improve the standard. The manager of the quarry had a house beside the Guest House and he allowed us to use a room as a store for our Red Cross parcels. These changes raised our standard of living a bit. We didn't have a football pitch but we had a ball and space to kick it about in. In summer weather we enjoyed the relaxation of sitting outside, a facility not available at Lichtovitz.

When we came to Lichtovitz from Stalag IVB, we were only a handful of bewildered men with an N.C.O. - a Sergeant - as the Senior Rank. We were a mixed bunch from a miscellany of Service Units and from an even greater variety of backgrounds in Civvy Street. During my brief stay at Stalag IVB, I formed the impression that it was the equivalent of a POW H.Q. In fact, we had no contact with it and so we felt isolated.

In any case we were still in a pretty traumatic state and worrying about leisure activities was far from our minds. It was a difficult period and counselling for "Post Battle Trauma" was unheard of in 1942. I can just imagine the Commandant's expression if we had downed tools and asked for counselling!

The worst part of the winter was over. Despite the difficult conditions initially, we were now quite well organised and, if we were low in body and soul, at least we were coping with the work at the quarry face.

The increase in our numbers was due to the arrival of a Cypriot contingent and I'll write later about my relations with them in my capacity as Vertrauensmann.

When the Red Cross provided us with new uniforms, I was surprised at my reaction to wearing the British Army khaki again. When I first saw myself in khaki I was very unimpressed but after months of feeling bedraggled, I now felt quite smart in my khaki. Perversely, I was loth to part with the old clothes that I kept as working togs. It gave me quite a boost to look smart when the occasion arose. When the colder weather came, it was too cold to think of being smart.

I was even more surprised when the Commandant gave permission for photographs to be taken to send home. We put on our best bibs and tuckers and smiled as though we were in a Butlins camp. Some of the lads thought that we should not make the folks at home think that we were being treated like lords but most of us were pleased that our families would be relieved to see us looking so well.

I wondered about the Commandant's decision to allow photographs. No doubt he thought that it would give a good impression in Britain of the Germans' treatment of British POW's and that might please his superiors. On the other hand, the local German population, suffering badly through rationing of clothes and food, already resented the marvellous Red Cross parcels, and they might be even more resentful to see us in bright new uniforms.

Escapes

Our stay at Stalag IVB had not been long enough for us fully to realise that from now on we would spend most of our time fenced in behind that accursed barbed wire. I wrote above about the organised leisure activities at Lamsdorf. It was considerably later that I learned about the highly developed organisations in the large Stalags and Oflags devoted entirely to planning and executing escapes.

The Stalags had sufficient Senior NCO's to take charge and to form Escape Committees to ensure that only well planned escapes would be allowed. All plans for an escape had to be submitted to that committee. Every plan was subjected to close examination to ensure it was feasible and that all the logistics had been worked out. Approved plans went on a waiting list, the position on the list depending on the likelihood of its success. The committee would have funds and materials to support an approved plan and it must have been an enormous boost to morale even to be planning an escape. I speak from memory of what I was told so I may not have all the details correct.

The possibility of escaping from our small camp was discussed, but initially, the question of anything organised was never really considered. Our situation was quite different from that in a Stalag. In the first place, when we arrived at Lichtovitz we were still in a poor physical condition. After a day's work we were so exhausted that it took us all our time to get to bed, far less envisage the demands of a realistic escape plan.

Later on, when some were fit enough to think about the possibilities of escape, a deterrent was the fact that the chance of success was remote. Admittedly we would have had no need to dig tunnels, with all the problems that entailed. It was quite feasible to get away from the quarry and, with a bit of luck, your absence might not have been observed until the roll call before we left it. Compared to a Stalag organisation that would be about our only plus point.

Against it were all the minuses. Our only outside contacts from whom we might obtain clothes, maps, etc. were the few workers at the Quarry and there were so few POWs that raising money to fund such a project would be difficult. The camp was a long, long distance from Switzerland, the only realistic avenue of escape from Czechoslovakia. Switzerland's narrow mountain passes made Border security easy for the Germans to supervise.

A few of us had a smattering of German but no knowledge of the Slav language. If we had civilian clothes we might have passed off as compulsory labourers from occupied countries and that could have helped with the language problem. Czechoslovakia was an occupied country so the place was hoaching with suspicious officials forever stopping people for their papers. Finding escapees from a British POW camp would result in organised searches and, even if you had civilian clothes, the lack of papers would make for an early capture.

You would have to travel at night and walk all the way to Switzerland, a journey of several hundred miles and any food that you carried would be consumed in no time.

A Czech found guilty of assisting escaping POW's would be severely punished and perhaps their families as well, so it would be asking a lot to expect them to help. The Czechs would, no doubt, be sympathetic, but they could not be expected to be willing. They were, after all, under the thumb of the Germans who would hand out horrendous punishment to the entire family of any man who assisted the enemy.

Even if you could find anyone willing to help, you could never be sure that they were not Quislings. [Quisling was an infamous Norwegian who collaborated with the Germans in their occupation of his country and his name became eponymous for all collaborators].

If things went wrong for an escapee the greatest risk of being shot was at the point of capture. If you were in civilian clothes, the Germans could shoot you on sight, no questions asked. Your luck would depend on the attitude of your captors. Many Germans hated the British enough to have no qualms about shooting on sight. The resentment shown to our Red Cross parcels was well known in areas near POW camps and that could easily turn to hate in an escape.

I thoroughly hated being a POW, so I would have accepted the dangers of being caught provided that there was a reasonable chance of success, but the odds against a successful escape from Czechoslovakia through Switzerland were exceptionally high.

I asked myself, what would be the real purpose of planning to escape from Lichtovitz? It would certainly not be because there was a reasonable chance of getting away. It could be a feeling that it was a duty to escape. That was a strong feeling for some. It had to be very strong to go over the wire regardless of the possibility of success or of

The Two Escapees. Harry (left) and Mike.

the odds on being shot in the attempt.

Others had simply reached the mental stage when they could no longer stand incarceration and would rather accept any odds on being caught rather than bear being behind barbed wire any longer.

I could sympathise with the latter. I decided that the odds were too high in the present situation for a fruitless failure. However, if I were ever moved to another camp where the chance of success was reasonable, I would certainly go over the wire.

As far as I know, there was only one attempt to escape from Praskovitz but I was away at the time and I did not hear the details from the lads involved, Harry Schofield and Mike Mycock. I was told that they were captured not far from Praskovitz. They were both good lads whose company and friendship I had enjoyed and appreciated. They were both intelligent and I feel that they must have found a method that had a good chance of success. Although the escape was not successful, I know that they would be glad that they made the effort. I do hope that they came to no harm.

Sex

Not having ever contemplated entering a monastery, I was unprepared for years of monastic celibacy. For long periods I was certainly celibate, but not from choice I hasten to say.

On the convoy I was almost introduced to a form of sex about which I was completely innocent and when in Egypt I turned down the opportunity of enhancing my sex education at a brothel. During the Battle of Crete I had neither inclination nor opportunity.

For a long time, during that march in Crete and on the train journey to Germany, thoughts of sex were completely subordinated to surviving the awful conditions. After the Red Cross parcels arrived and improved our diet, my hunger abated a little and the constant tiredness eased off. I noticed that my libido was beginning to perk up and that something was stirring deep down that was not diarrhoea! I realised then that sex awareness is related to eating well. Unfortunately, strong sexual awareness, linked to no opportunity over a long period, was extremely frustrating. For some that frustration was too much and they took terrible risks of severe punishment.

At Praskovitz an opportunity arose for me - well, more than the opportunity arose. The manager of the quarry had two young daughters. Our store for Red Cross parcels was an extension of their house and I noticed that my occasional visits to the store increasingly coincided with the lassies coming in to the room on some specious pretext or other. My German was not all that good but the German language was less important than that other language - body language.

I was undecided whether I was interpreting that language correctly - since the lassies were frequently more attracted to our parcels than they were to us - until confirmation arrived by way of a nice warm hand caressing my shoulder. My knees had not been so shaky since Crete. Before I could respond to this call for action stations, we heard the noise of footsteps on the stone floor of the corridor. It could have been the quarry manager so ardour on both sides rapidly disappeared.

151

Another case of my "Almosts"?

There was good reason for my ardour being dampened at the prospect of the quarry manager walking into the room. The Germans had a way of discouraging randy males.

Apparently the following warning appeared on the Lamsdorf notice board: "Sexual intercourse with any females is verboten. Intercourse with a German girl is punishable by death." That seemed a wee bit drastic for that moment of ecstasy.

But many other cases were quoted, underlining that the Germans were not bluffing. When I first heard that POW's could be given a jail sentence for having sex with their pure Aryan girls, it seemed to me that a jail sentence was not much of a deterrent. After all a POW was already sentenced to imprisonment and doing hard labour on poor rations. It would be more or less just a change of environment. The death sentence changed my view and, as the quarry manager was an ardent Nazi, I decided to calm my ardour. I might have been dying for sex, but not in the literal sense, so I decided that a monastic existence for the duration was my lot. There ended my pitiful sex story.

The War Situation Improves

In the latter part of 1942 we heard a rumour that the Allies had landed an invasion force at Dieppe in France but it had been repelled, with heavy casualties. That was very depressing but it turned out to be German propaganda. Dieppe was a raid, not an invasion – disastrous, but at least not an unsuccessful invasion. That scarce commodity, good news, came towards the end of 1942.

Snippets of news percolated through from camps that had a secret wireless and could listen to the BBC World Service. The news that Rommel's army in the Desert was in retreat cheered us up no end and was marvellous for morale. The MNBDO was intended to support the defence of Tobruck and I hoped that, if my comrades who were evacuated from Crete were posted there, they had all survived.

The other item of good news was the one that we had waited for so long in vain to hear. The German Army had advanced to Stalingrad, but had been halted outside the city. Although it seemed that the odds were against their sweeping advances in Russia being stopped, I had tried to stay optimistic ever since the surrender on Crete. I did my best to fight against a pessimistic question that lurked just below the surface. If Germany conquered the whole of Western Europe, might I be incarcerated in one form or another for the rest of my life?

At last I could put to rest that niggling and cancerous thought, no matter the length of the tunnel, a light now shone at the end of it. The uplift was tremendous. On receipt of that marvellous news about Stalingrad, pessimism disappeared like 'snaw aff a dyke'. It was replaced by a surge of optimism, hopefully not premature.

I thought of my earlier hope that Hitler's army might over-reach themselves, and that, like Napoleon, they would be forced to retreat. Next winter, when the freezing cold numbed my fingers, I took heart that the sub zero temperatures in Russia might yet defeat Hitler and prove our saviour. The will to survive whatever the immediate future might throw at me was now strengthened as this optimism crept in.

Barbed Wire Madness

Perhaps I gave the impression of over-reacting when I referred so often to the strength of my feelings about the "Barbed Wire Madness". But the reality of it was sadly evidenced by the news from hospital of a friend's suicide. I was utterly shattered.

Joe had been unwell for a time and I knew that the stress and frustration of being closed in had affected him more than most. I did not hear how it happened but I could guess that all his feelings of frustration and the apparent hopelessness of his situation had built up to an intolerable pressure point.

I too had looked down the dark tunnel of incarceration and, although I may have wavered at times, I clung like grim death to the belief that one day I would be back home roaming freely around my beloved Scotland. Joe must also have looked down the tunnel but saw no light at the end, only darkness, a black, black darkness that eventually overwhelmed him.

If I had only been with him when he reached that lonely and desperate stage, I would have held out a hand for him to cling to. How little we know of the tortuous battles being fought, and oft times lost, in the minds of those around us. When we do find out, it is often too late, much too late to hold out the helping hand.

I thought hard then about our attitude to all the things that cumulatively made our life so difficult since we first became POW's, poor physical conditions, hunger (perhaps it was almost starvation). In my opinion the "Barbed Wire Madness" was arguably worse than all these other deprivations.

In our small and isolated community we had nobody to turn to for assistance or guidance, so we had to work out our own way of handling psychological problems. The sad suicide underlined the strength of our depressive emotions.

Hunger provoked the first depressive emotion and we conjured up visions of beautiful food. When our meal of watery gravy and a mouse - like portion of meat was dished up, someone was bound to say something like: "Oh! What I could do to a nice steak pie with rich thick gravy, roast potatoes and Yorkshire Pudding, followed by apple pie and custard." After a while this drove some round the bend and anyone going on about super food was told to shut up.

The same treatment was given to anyone constantly going on about being closed in at nights and being driven daft by "Barbed Wire Madness". Strangely enough, although sex was probably the strongest and most difficult of emotions to control, the subject of sex was never seriously discussed. An immense variety of sexy jokes were told and I thought at the time that submersion was the best way to handle this subject.

The fact that, for a long time, there was no foreseeable end to the

War made depression the most serious problem of a POW's existence. Nowadays we are told that bottling up strong emotions is wrong. Would our colleague have stepped back from the brink if he had lived to hear the good news about Stalingrad? We shall never know. Perhaps I was wrong to bottle up my phobia about incarceration but it never crossed my mind to take such a drastic action as my unfortunate comrade.

Cypriots

The arrival of the Cypriot soldiers increased our numbers to about fifty. They were very cheerful fellows. They came from the Turkish part of Cyprus. They spoke little English and only a few could read so their request for me to act as their Vertrauensmann in their dealings with the Germans gave me yet more language problems.

But the first problem did not require a knowledge of German. Their religion prohibited certain foods and they sometimes did not know the contents of the tins in the Red Cross parcels. Unfortunately a few took advantage of this. If the lads fancied a particular tin of meat, they would say: "Not that tin, your religion forbids it." and then swap it for an item they did not fancy. We soon sorted that out.

I grew to like the Cypriots very much and I learned a lot about their culture and their customs, of which eating communally was one. They shared all their food and sat together at the same table, putting the food in the middle and helping themselves to whatever they wanted. I was very impressed with their discipline because there were no arguments and nobody ever tried to eat the lion's share.

Another small problem involving food arose when I was privileged to be invited to join their table for a meal. They had persuaded the cook to give them large platters to accommodate their preference for sharing. The food was beautifully arranged around the platter but one of the items caused me a moment of anxiety. The edge of the plate was decorated with small animals and their wee heads were hanging down

**Four Cypriot Comrades From the Royal Army Transport Corps.
Balih Yusuh, the Cypriots' leader, above right.**

the outside. I could not identify the animal. I was not sure whether you ate the whole beastie, head and all, or whether one selected from the varied number of items on the plate in a certain order.

I now know that it was their custom not to start until their guest chose. I decided to act as if I was daft, pointing to the side of my head, picking up one of the wee beasties and making it walk round the plate. There was silence for a moment and I was aghast in case I had insulted them in some way.

If I did offend them the leader, Balih Yusuh, with typical Eastern hospitality, ignored my peculiar habits, shook his head, pointed to his mouth and ate his portion before I did – a simple solution, why didn't I think of it? They all laughed at the mad Scotsman and tucked into the meal.

The real problem, however, was that the wee beasties were hedgehogs, a rare delicacy in Cyprus but, unfortunately, it was strictly against the law in Germany to kill them. The evidence quickly disappeared but not from any sense of disposing of the incriminating evidence but because they tasted nice, with a very delicate flavour and texture like a young chicken.

The introduction of a new group with a different language and culture was very refreshing. Even my task as interpreter took on a new lease of life because I had to concentrate on making myself understood. I also was very interested to hear about their life in Cyprus and they were equally engrossed in my tales about Scotland, although I was stuck for a word to explain the kilt without calling it a skirt. We Scots have a thing about the kilt being called a skirt but I needn't have bothered because they were accustomed to seeing the Greek and Cretan men wearing a skirt. I was given many photographs but they omitted to give their addresses so I did not keep up the association after the war.

More news of the War

The year 1942 drew to a close and sometime in the New Year we heard news that really had us jumping for joy. Now the German army was not only retreating from Stalingrad but also the remnants of their force had surrendered. We could scarcely contain ourselves but we had to be exceptionally careful not to let the Germans have any suspicions of the cause of our jubilation. If we kept telling them news that they only heard about much later, they would become suspicious. Our news was second hand and belated but it was accurate, whereas the news that the Germans heard from their wireless seldom was.

Goebbels, the German Minister responsible for disseminating propaganda, was not renowned for giving accurate information if the news was bad for Germans' morale.

The Czechs told us that the local Germans were becoming very worried about the course of the war. If the news that the Germans had been halted at Stalingrad had us jumping for joy, we could have jumped over the moon when we got the news that they were actually retreating. News like that had an immediate effect on our outlook for the future.

The War situation for the Germans deteriorated in 1943 and the possibility that, as they retreated, the fanatical element in the German forces would carry out scorched earth tactics, caused some concern.

The people from the occupied countries, the Czechs and Poles, had even more cause for concern and not only from the Germans but also from the Russians. The news of defeats and retreats was affecting the morale of the civilian population.

Simultaneously the conditions in Germany were deteriorating and food rationing grew even tighter. The black market thrived in these conditions but even those who normally could afford these prices were feeling the pinch. I got a lot of information about the feelings of the Czechs from Jan, my fellow worker at the quarry. He warned me to look out for Czechs who might be aggressive because of rumours that

POW's were dealing with the racketeers in the black market.

Considering the hardships that they were suffering, it would be surprising if the German population did not feel some animosity towards us. We, after all, were the enemy and if rumour had it that we were living off the fat of the land through the Red Cross parcels, their resentment was bound to increase. I would have felt the same in their position.

The third year of our incarceration, 1943, was uneventful so far as life at the quarry and the prison camp was concerned. The steadily worsening food situation still affected us but the regular parcels certainly helped a lot. Fresh food was in scarce supply.

The news from the Stalag was slow in percolating down but it was all the sweeter when it came. The war situation in 1943 and 1944 was not good, particularly the news that Japan had attacked Pearl Harbour, although that was good news in so far as it resulted in the Americans entering the war.

The news that the USA had entered the European scene and had joined with Britain to make a successful landing in France lifted the roof off the ceiling. The Germans were now in retreat on all fronts, France, the North African Desert, Russia and Italy. The prospects now were so good that my mind focused all the time on the marvellous thought that the war might come to an end sooner than I had expected.

With the vision of going home now in front of me, the unbearable thought that incarceration might be infinite was no longer uppermost in my mind. The war situation for the Allies was improving all the time. The news for the German Army was invariably bad and their morale was badly dented. The morale of the civilians was also low. A festering situation developed and their fear that the Russians would arrive before the Allies was beginning to show more and more.

In our remote rural area the danger of physical assault from the Germans had been minimal up until now but that could all change. I had no illusions about our fate if we happened to be in the path of the retreating Army. We hoped that we would get enough warning before that situation arose. The ordinary German civilians and local soldiers were unlikely to take such action because they would be as terrified of Russian reprisals as the Czechs. When Germany surrendered, the people of the occupied countries would pray that the Allies would free them.

The British Free Corps

In view of the war situation, I was flabbergasted when a pamphlet from the Germans was distributed in our camp. A Unit calling itself the British Free Corps was inviting us to join. We had not heard even a whisper that such a Unit had been formed. Who were these people who were alleged to have received repeated applications from all parts of the world and where were they?

If they were POW's in Germany, they could hardly call themselves free. Why had we not seen them or heard about them? In the tight environment of a prison camp, a subject like that could not be kept a secret for long. The pamphlet would require the collaboration of the Germans and the conspirators would be lucky to get out of a prison camp alive.

Admittedly we were at the back of beyond but we did get items of news coming out of the Stalags. Surely the lads in the Stalag would do their utmost to let us know something as explosive as that as soon as possible. I noted that whoever was responsible for the pamphlet had not dared to reveal his identity - neither a name nor a title. If he were British and a POW he would be too scared.

The punctuation on the pamphlet was chaotic so I wondered if perhaps the writer were not British. There is much more about the British Free Corps in Chapter 9 and at Appendix A. A scanned copy of the original pamphlet is on the following page. It may not be too legible, however, because, like me, it has suffered the ravages of time.

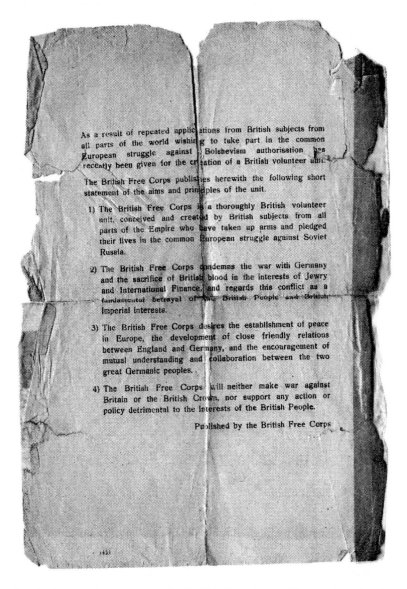

As a result of repeated applications from British subjects from all parts of the world wishing to take part in the common European struggle against Bolshevism authorisation has recently been given for the creation of a British volunteer unit.

The British Free Corps publishes herewith the following short statement of the aims and principles of the unit.

1) The British Free Corps is a thoroughly British volunteer unit, conceived and created by British subjects from all parts of the Empire who have taken up arms and pledged their lives in the common European struggle against Soviet Russia.

2) The British Free Corps condemns the war with Germany and the sacrifice of British blood in the interests of Jewry and International Finance, and regards this conflict as a fundamental betrayal of the British People and British Imperial Interests.

3) The British Free Corps desires the establishment of peace in Europe, the development of close friendly relations between England and Germany, and the encouragement of mutual understanding and collaboration between the two great Germanic peoples.

4) The British Free Corps will neither make war against Britain or the British Crown, nor support any action or policy detrimental to the interests of the British People.

Published by the British Free Corps

Original pamphlet issued by the British Free Corps. Note written by the Author on the back of the pamphlet when he received it: "This audacious pamphlet was issued to the British Prisoners of War at Praskovitz, Sudetenland, on Tuesday, 23rd May, 1944".

Chapter 9

Berlin

Genshagen

About the middle of 1944, the Commandant intimated that the Fuhrer had agreed to show his appreciation for all the POW's who had worked in salt mines, coal mines and stone quarries by allowing a camp to be opened in Berlin where they could have a well earned rest.

At first we thought that our humourless Commandant had found a sense of humour from somewhere. When we recovered from the shock of being the recipient of appreciation from his beloved Fuhrer, we listened intently. He said our camp had been chosen to send one POW to attend the rest camp.

The Fuhrer's feelings of appreciation must have been one of the best kept secrets of the war. The thousands of POW's captured since Dunkirk would have said that there were plenty of feelings expressed towards them over the years but never a feeling that could, by any stretch of the imagination, be described as appreciative. I am sure that the Fuhrer would have been hurt if he had known just how long it had taken for his feelings towards us to percolate down to our level.

We discussed at length what possible reasons there could be for this move. Could the Germans be preparing for defeat and was this a gesture to appease the British after the war? It did not seem to be in keeping with their image.

We had no means of ascertaining the credentials of this camp in Berlin, another example of the disadvantage of a remote location with no means of communication. After discussion, the consensus of opinion was that there could be no harm in someone going to Berlin to find out and report back as to whether it was genuine. At least one person would have a most desirable rest from breaking up stones.

It was proposed that it would have to be someone who could be trusted and whose judgement would be accepted, and I was flattered to be asked whether I would tackle the task. I gave it a lot of consideration because I would have preferred more information before deciding. If only I could have had a contact with the Stalag but there was no channel of communication with them.

I still could not fathom out why the Germans should suddenly be so concerned to give a rest to those whom they had forced into hard labour for years under terrible conditions.

It seemed to me that there were two points in favour of going:
(1) at least I would not be working for the Germans for that period;
(2) that Berlin was much closer to the West and, if the security in a rest camp was slacker than a normal camp, an opportunity might arise to make a successful escape.

I facetiously said to my colleagues that I had decided to accept their proposal that I go because the promotion prospects at the quarry were not good enough. I was told to be ready to travel at short notice. With the amount of clobber that I had, I barely needed five minutes notice.

One morning I was told that a guard had arrived to escort me to Berlin. It was a strange feeling as I walked out the camp gate. I was leaving behind colleagues with whom I had been in very close contact for years and with whom I had made very good friends. For a POW the immediate or long-term future was always unpredictable and I might never see them again.

I was going on what was called a holiday but it was unlike any other holiday imaginable. I doubted that I would be whooping it up at a Butlin's holiday camp. A Red Coat standing by with a Spandau machine gun would somehow spoil that image.

I was still very unsure what lay ahead but it would certainly be an experience. Whatever will be will be! As I stepped into the carriage of the train to Berlin, my thoughts went back to my last train journey. This was a bit more comfortable but an armed guard by my side reminded me that freedom was still some distance away.

Otherwise there was no comparison. Incoming passengers looked at me with curiosity but I could see their anxiety (perhaps fear would be a more apt description) as they rapidly averted their gaze when they saw an armed guard at my side. Most of them moved to another compartment and I was tempted to let out a loud bellow to new people who came in, just to underline how dangerous I was. It might have given me the luxury of empty seats on which to stretch out my legs for the rest of the journey.

The journey was not as long as I expected. The German Government's sponsored tour of Europe had now taken me through four capital Cities. The first three visits were non-stop except for the brief wait at a platform in Budapest. We arrived at Berlin but, like the other Capitals, I saw little of it

We travelled through the city to the outskirts. In Praskovitz we had been far removed from any bombing raids by the RAF and we were not even on a flight path. I was taken aback, therefore, to see the amount of destruction here. It dawned on me that, after surviving bombing by the Germans in Britain and again in Crete, I could now be in danger in Berlin of being bombed by the RAF. How ironic that would be.

When I saw the tremendous destruction, I realised that the death toll must have been very high. Why on earth, I asked myself, would the Germans keep on sending POW's to a rest camp, particularly a camp situated near to the capital city where the casualties were so high?

We arrived at our destination, the guard said "Genshagen". There were no fairy lights around the perimeter and no lovely female Red Coats to welcome me and wish me a happy holiday. There was just the same old barbed wire around it to provide a homely touch and remind me of Praskovitz. At Praskovitz the guard had popped in and out on various pretexts but this was more like a Stalag with a guardhouse and armed guards on the perimeter. It looked like any normal POW camp and why not? Despite its purpose, it still was a POW camp.

The welcome from the POW camp management team could not have been better. I was introduced to John Brown, nicknamed Busty, the camp leader and a Q.M., a Senior N.C.O. rank in the Royal Artillery. His assistants were Reg. Beattie, Administration, Tony Abraham, Assistant to Reg. Beattie, Jimmy Newcombe, Canteen, and Ian Ryburn, a New Zealander and a lay preacher.

They all came from Blechhammer, a large working camp with around 5000 men. That sounded more like a small town compared to our wee camp at Praskovitz. I was wide eyed as they told me of the facilities at Blechhammer. It had a large canteen, a library, a camp magazine, an orchestra and a huge supply of sporting equipment, There were so many nationalities that they could hold international football matches. They had sufficient musicians to form Bands and to give musical shows.

I was dizzy with amazement and I could appreciate why John Brown and his Blechhammer colleagues had been chosen to run a holiday camp. I wrote earlier that we felt isolated at Praskovitz and that we had practically no leisure facilities. Even if we had leisure facilities such as there were at Genshagen, we would often have been too tired after work to take advantage of them. I had no feelings of envy, just astonishment at the scale of it all. Indeed, my thought was that, although the marvellous leisure facilities made a pleasant break in the monotony of prison life, they in no way compensated for the four years since Dunkirk that most of these lads had endured behind barbed wire.

I was hoping to hear something at this initial "Introduction" that would answer my big question, namely, why on earth did the Germans decide to keep on this rest camp at a time when their armies were in retreat on all fronts? There was no doubt about the sincerity and friendliness of John Brown and his staff. The fact that they had learned a lot about managing and presenting leisure activities at Blechhammer was obvious from the impressive programme of activities for our visit, a task not enhanced by the barbed wire and the armed guards.

I doubt whether they had a clue about life at our wee working camp. Brown tried to create a relaxed atmosphere that indicated that he appreciated that most of the POW visitors had been through a rough time. I was also impressed that we were not expected to jump up in the morning ready for a hectic and active day. They appreciated that some of their intake might benefit from doing absolutely nothing. After three years without a break of going to work at the quarry face I enjoyed just plain mucking about with no guards shouting orders at you. I really did enjoy the pleasure of using the facilities, particularly the Library.

It was really interesting to listen to the experiences of stories of POW's from all over Germany. We swapped yarns about how and where we were captured and drew comparisons with life in our respective working camps.

I chummed up with a fellow Scot, Benny McLaughlin. Benny had a great sense of humour and he and I became very good friends He asked about my job in Civvy Street. I told him that I was a Sorting Clerk in the Glasgow Post Office, parcels being the heaviest thing I had to lift. Compared to that, I had found work at the quarry face very tough. "You're lucky," he replied, "my work down a coal mine in Allanton in Lanarkshire was hard enough, although I didnae mind the hard work. I would have loved a job in the open air but with a' the unemployment, ye had to tak any job ye could get." When War broke out Benny joined the Army, the Black Watch. He was very glad to leave the mines behind and it was a joy, he said, to be out in the open air. "Where are you working now?" I asked. "I didnae have awfie long in the open air," Benny said. "The bastards put me down the salt mines". I thought how cruel life can be.

Sport

The organisation and the facilities were quite good. Football was my major sport so I was delighted to see a football pitch and to learn that there were usually enough people interested to form at least two teams. Other sports included volleyball, a new sport for me, played on a sanded court. Athletics was popular and a track was made around the centre of the camp. Quite a few athletic events were held and they attracted a good number of spectators.

Fitness for athletics and the fitness engendered by hard labour are quite different. I started to do a bit of running and other exercises now that I did not have to wield a sledgehammer daily. An athletic event was being planned and someone suggested that I should enter for the mile.

I never did shine at athletics. My training was aimed at speed bursts for football. The marathon is the recognised long distance race. For me anything over 440 yards was a marathon. Against my better judgement I let my name go forward. I was reasonably fit but my idea of a well-planned mile-run was one where stopping for the odd cup of tea was acceptable.

I banked on most of the other runners being more familiar with other events, such as darts, dominoes and quaffing beer. The event created a lot of interest and it reached my ears that the lads were placing bets on the race. What was worse, I heard my name mentioned. On the big occasion, as I lined up for the off, I spotted someone whose presence I did not expect at an athletic event. He was a lean and wiry specimen so it should not have surprised me that he used to be an athlete but he was partial to cigarettes and was not so fit now.

As we lined up at the start, I had not a clue about the strategy of running a mile race. I set off at a fair pace, hoping that the majority would drop out with the unaccustomed excess of energy. At the third lap I was going, not strong, just going. The lungs and the legs were reminding me that I had trained them for short sharp bursts and that they wanted to call it a day. To my astonishment and chagrin the heavy smoker whizzed past as if he had just started. A good athlete would have responded immediately but although the spirit was strong the legs were not. In other words, I packed up. My friend won the race at a canter with nobody in sight. At least he hadn't a fag in his mouth when he passed me!

The sporting activities were a panacea for me and after a week I began to relax. I had not realised just how tense I had become in the working camp. Although there was still that barbed wire perimeter and guards outside it, there was a relaxed atmosphere inside the camp. Apart from security issues, there was no doubt that John Brown was in complete charge of the running of the camp and of organising the activities. John had also been allowed to select his management staff.

He made a wise choice in selecting Ian Ryburn, the lay preacher. When I talked to POW's from other camps, I was interested to hear that "Barbed Wire Madness" was widespread in all of them. A lot of the men were suffering from it. I was pleased to be told that it now was recognised in the big Stalags as something that badly needed attention. In a small working camp there was nobody qualified who could listen and objectively help with your problem.

Ian Ryburn was just the person who could do that and he brought great comfort to many. He had been through the mill in Crete. I wrote about the New Zealand soldiers who were captured in the fight to hold Maleme Airport. A New Zealand Unit was holding a position outside the airport. The Germans advanced to attack it and they placed the captured soldiers in front of themselves as a shield. I was told that Ian had been one of them. Typically he never mentioned it to me.

Entertainment

I mentioned the variety, standard and quality of the entertainment laid on at Genshagen, a relatively small camp. The influence of John Brown's contacts at Blechhammer was obvious. I was in the last party to come to Genshagen but I heard that the Bands and the Blechhammer Dramatic Society had been to Genshagen and presented a production of the Mikado, a really professional performance.

While I was there the staff and visiting POW's put on a number of variety shows. Most of the costumes for these shows were hand-made. My new friend, Benny McLaughlin, was involved in several of the variety turns. He had been given a good grounding in Highland dancing in the Black Watch and one of his showpieces was the famous Sword Dance. He endeavoured to pass on his skills to me. I had seen it danced often but I did not realise the complications of the dance. It was with great reluctance, therefore, that I agreed to Benny's suggestion that we perform it together in one of the variety shows.

I was liable to make a mess of the show and I suggested that it might turn out to be a comedy turn. Benny told me that in serious presentations of the sword dance in byegone days, the blades were laid down with the edge upwards. I was so glad that this ancient practice was no longer observed, otherwise I would have finished up legless. The kilts were made from bed sheets. They were way above the regulation height, exposing very bony (not bonny) knees.

If there were any Black Watch dance instructors in the audience, Benny might have been court-martialled for his appearance in a kilt that looked more like a mini skirt. A performance by two of the cast from Blechhammer as drag artists would have done credit to any professional show.

Scenes from some of these shows are portrayed in the following pages:

Author back left. Benny at front right

Ian Drysdale left,
Benny right. Kilts
made from bed
sheets.

The camp Dachshund being taught to say "Hande Hoch".

Sports staff. The Author (extreme right) sits beside Benny. Reg Beattie at back.

Cast of variety show

Scenes from The Mikado. Produced by the Dramatic Society of the Blechhammer POW camp.

Fancy dress at Genshagen, Berlin, 1944.

Another feature that came to Genshagen before my arrival was the well-equipped orchestra from Blechhammer. The number of musicians in it was greater than the number of POW's at Praskovitz. It was the last thing I expected in a POW camp.

Education would not be considered entertainment by a lot of people but someone had the bright idea that many of the POW's would appreciate lessons on speaking German. I jumped at the chance of learning more of the language. Our teacher was very high-class, a Professor of Languages at the Heidelberg University. Ye Gods! Free lessons from the Oxford of Germany.

I had visions of returning to Praskovitz with a posh German accent but I climbed down from that fantasy at the very beginning. He asked whether anyone had any German at all. Nobody had the gall to answer but a bright spark said: "Alex Clark is an interpreter." As there wasn't a hole in the floor to jump into I had to stand up and explain the truth behind that exaggeration.

He persuaded me to say a few words and his first comment was to ask me to which part of Britain I belonged. I told him that I belonged to Glasgow. I was tempted to say "A' belong tae Glesga', dear old Glesga toon," but I decided that interpreting my German would be enough for the Professor to cope with in one session.

His next comment was: "Well, Alex, your English has a nice Scottish accent. Would you be surprised to learn that you have an equally rustic Bavarian accent? He made it sound like a compliment so I didn't tell him that (a) Glaswegians are not considered rustic and (b) an Austrian taught me my first few words. Maybe the Austrian had Bavarian grandparents.

The professor ran into problems. A number in the class might not have been aware that it was a language class because their English was not too good. The Professor recognised this quite soon when his efforts to explain German grammar fell on stony ground. He suggested that it might be beneficial if he spent some time on English grammar first.

Nobby, one of the camp characters, had an accent that placed his birthplace right under Bow Bells. The Professor asked Nobby to read a piece from a book. The word three cropped up a few times and Nobby had a big problem with the pronunciation of the syllable "Th". He said "free" instead of "three". The Professor said: "Nobby, the word is pronounced "three" not "free". Nobby tried hard but failed at each attempt.

Nobby's patience broke and he burst out: "I'm f——g well saying 'free', ain't I". I believe that was the Professor's last lesson.

I was surprised that a visit to the famous Potsdam-Sanssouci Palace was planned. Thoughts of planning an escape entered my head when Berlin was mentioned but there was no time to prepare for that. The air raids on Berlin were quite frequent in 1944 and the Germans were still retreating on all Fronts. I expected that the Berliners would have

**Nobby, left, who said
"I'm saying f ——— free"**

considerable animosity towards British POW's.

The palace had escaped the bombers and it was an interesting and instructive visit, but I was even more interested in the tremendous destruction of the city. That was not a sight worth seeing. It was wartime, I know, and such destruction of civilian areas is part of modern war. I felt it was a sad commentary on the times that such massive destruction was the only solution to a problem.

Some of the facilities at Genshagen would have made my Praskovitz friends green with envy. Simple things like showers and a laundry room. Even more luxurious compared to, say, Lichtovitz, was a toilet, a real toilet with doors on – what a marvellous treat. Mind you, there still were no flushing facilities but even the Savoy Hotel wouldn't have made me feel better. Some of the lads were so taken with a proper toilet that did not have a hurricane blowing up their rear end that they sat in it for ages, reading a book.

Shoe repairing is not a utility that you would expect in a prison camp. A lad on one of the parties was a shoe repairer by trade and John Brown jumped at the opportunity to keep such a valuable asset. It was a much-appreciated service for many of the lads. Amazingly, some of them had not changed their boots since they were captured. The shoe repairer was in great demand.

This shoe repairer (I wish that I could remember his name. I'll call him Bill for this story.) had another function that perhaps excelled even his shoe repairing service. He had the responsibility of listening to the BBC World Service broadcasts. I had heard about this fantastic facility in large camps. Bill was persuaded to show me the wireless receiving equipment. I thought that the reception of a broadcast from Britain would require a fairly large piece of equipment and was interested to find out how such equipment could be hidden from the Germans.

Posting Benny to watch out, Bill casually reached up to his locker and took down a rectangular biscuit tin. He removed several layers of biscuits and carefully lifted out an instrument. Its wooden base had been made to fit exactly in the biscuit tin. When I saw it I could scarcely believe my eyes. It was a "Cat's Whisker" crystal wireless set, one of the earliest wireless receivers.

The last time I had seen a set like that was when I was a wee laddie in the 1920's. On a family visit to my Uncle John, he had announced with great pride that he had built something that would surprise us. He had constructed a Cat's Whisker wireless. Not many people had the knowledge to make a wireless or the means to afford such a luxury. Probably it was considered the latest high tech apparatus of these times but I was too small to understand the interest provoked by this new phenomenon.

My Uncle invited us to a demonstration of the new marvel. It was quite an occasion and my Aunt Kate laid out her usual lovely supper. We were told that all the cakes must be eaten before the big show started. She had a great sense of humour because we needed no "conditions" to persuade us to gobble them up despite my Mum's protestations. I sat near the set as Uncle John fiddled away with the wee handle that manoeuvred across the even smaller crystal. It seemed an eternity until he shouted: "I hear a voice."

In those days, when children were seen and not heard, the adults had first chance to listen. I could scarcely contain my excitement. I was sure that the wee man in the crystal would go away before my turn came. Then I heard a voice that sounded far away. I was only a bairn so I thought it must be magic. "Where is the man in the wee box," I asked? "Is he round the back?"

These memories flooded back as I renewed an acquaintance with a wee "Cat's Whisker" crystal set in this most unlikely place, a POW camp in Germany. Bill and his crystal set gave a service that boosted morale for thousands of POW's, perhaps more than anything else did.

The World Service must have been very powerful for that wee set to pick it up. The utmost care had to be taken not only to keep the set in a safe place but also to avoid spreading any news that would make the Germans suspicious. Bill told me that on one occasion when a snap search was mounted, the search party entered his room. A guard reached for the biscuit tin with the wireless in it. Bill, with great presence of mind, jumped up and quickly removed the lid. He offered one of them a biscuit.

His heart was in his mouth because, if they took more than two, it would reveal the wireless and the game was up. They both refused the offer, but were so pleased because Bill did not resent their search that they left without searching further. Thanks to Bill's presence of mind, we kept receiving our heart-warming news.

The future prospects for POW's grew brighter as the Allies advanced on all fronts. It took weeks or even months for news to percolate to Praskovitz whereas at Genshagen the news from the BBC World Service was updated daily from Bill's wireless. For example, news of D-Day, the Allies entering Rome and the Russians continuing to push the Germans back was available almost immediately.

In the early autumn we heard that the Allies had entered Reich territory. Unjustifiably I thought that the war might be over soon and I had a vision of spending Hogmanay 1944 at home. The worrying thoughts that our future might be forever under Nazi domination were long since gone. But there was still an anxiety. Now, as the German Army was pushed back into their own country, would the fanatical element pursue a do or die pogrom? I thought about it, particularly as Praskovitz was too far to the East for my liking. These were only passing thoughts because I was now so optimistic that the prospect of being home again occupied my mind.

The British Free Corps

The time arrived for our party to return to their respective camps. I was preparing myself for the return to Praskovitz when I was given a big surprise. John Brown called Benny McLaughlin and me to his office. He said that he was looking for two people to join the Genshagen staff. He had been quite impressed with us and offered us a post. We would be working with Reg Beattie who was in charge of the office administration. It would mean that we would not, meantime, return to our working camps. To Benny and I, the prospect of not returning to salt mines and stone quarries did not exactly fill us with sadness. My friendship with Benny had developed into such a strong relationship that we were considering making a request to be posted to the same camp when our party was due to return.

John Brown said that one reason he wanted us to stay on as members of staff was that he had a proposal to put to us. Although I cannot recall exactly what was said at the meeting, I do know that what was discussed was, for me, the most interesting and exciting prospect of my time in Germany.

John said he had a very important task for which he needed two men. He would have to trust them implicitly to do the job well. It would be fatal if the Germans got to hear about the plan and we must not breathe a word about it to anyone until the mission had been accomplished. We were all agog. I remember thinking that it sounded far too important a task for two ordinary blokes like Benny and me.

John assumed that we had heard of the British Free Corps. He said that he had managed to learn the names of the men at the top of the organisation and also the names of the few British POW's who had enlisted in it. He had drawn up a plan to get this information out of Germany and he needed two men whom he could trust to act as couriers. There was a big element of risk but John considered that the plan had a good chance of success.

A German Officer, in whom he had complete trust, had to get away from Germany as soon as possible and he had agreed to act as an escort for the couriers. Arrangements had been made for the Officer to take us to the Front Line on the French border and either get us through the lines or show us where to get through. Miniature documents had been created with the information. They would be hidden in a secret compartment in the heels of our boots. He asked us if we would volunteer. We had no hesitation. For years I had said that I would not try to escape unless the plan at least had a reasonable chance of success. So far no plans discussed with me had been anything but an attempt to escape just for the sake of saying that you had done it. I had hoped that Berlin would provide a real opportunity. Now I was being offered not only a well-prepared plan with full back up but also good chance of success and a real purpose to motivate it. I could hardly wait for the call to go.

The adrenaline was flowing fast when I walked away from that meeting. The word ESCAPE in big capital letters was etched in my mind. Now an organised escape was being thrown in my lap. I had had absolutely no doubts about accepting the task when asked, but once I was back in my hut I began to think about some of the implications.

I realised, for instance, that I had not asked John anything about the Free Corps. To have obtained the names of members, it was obvious that John had either a contact in the Free Corps or had access to someone who knew all about it. I thought about the pamphlet from the British Free Corps that I received in Praskovitz and I pondered on that for a while. I deliberated on the possibility that John had a connection with them. I had formed the impression on my first contacts with John Brown that he was an open and honest sort of bloke. I am a great believer that the impressions you have of people when you first meet them are generally accurate. I had seen nothing that made me change my mind and I still had trust and faith in him. After all, it was he who told me that he had collected information about the Free Corps and he had no need to tell me anything.

There are times when you follow your instincts in taking a decision. My instincts told me that he would not let me down. I decided that the politics of the Free Corps were not my concern. After all, they had enlisted in the German Army. They were traitors prepared to fight for the enemy. The pamphlet stated that they would not fight against Britain. If circumstances arose that the Germans desperately needed reinforcements for an attack on the Allies, I wouldn't give them a chance in hell if they refused. Benny also trusted John Brown implicitly and had no qualms at all. It did occur to me that if the plan failed and the documents were revealed we might be classed as spies. I felt that it was a risk worth taking.

We watched Bill, the shoe repairer, making the cavity in the heel of our boots. After he finished the job, he had to work on the leather to make it look well worn. Time was passing and we heard no further details. We were only pawns in the plan so we couldn't go about making enquiries and we just had to be patient. That was difficult.

Every day we heard news on the wireless of further changes in the front line in France and we hoped that these changes would not affect our plan. Benny and I had been given no more details of the modus operandi of the break through the Front Line. I considered the possibility that we could be left on our own if something happened to our German escort. For obvious reasons, the camp library had no maps. I decided to ask John Brown, when he returned, for a briefing

Benny McLaughlin, with Bill, the shoe repairer. The secret documents about the British Free Corps being placed in a cavity in the heels. The Author and Benny planned to escape to France with the documents that incriminated Lord Haw Haw who was hanged for treason after the war.

on the logistics of the escape so that Benny and I could make our own contingency plans if we should be left on our own. I appreciated that John might be reluctant to give us names and other details of handing over the documents until the escape plan was ready to be implemented. All my thoughts now were centred on the escape.

Air Raids

In the meantime the escalation of the Allied bombing kept us occupied. There had been constant air raids on Berlin since my arrival at Genshagen. Before I arrived, the camp had been severely hit and a fair amount of damage done. I thought that I had had my fair share of bombing. Crete was considered by some to have been the heaviest concentration of the war. I am not certain of the exact period when Berlin was subjected to a massive night and day bombardment but I was at Genshagen in the summer and autumn of 1944 when it started.

The Daimler-Benz factory was about a mile from Genshagen and it was bound to be a target. Genshagen was on the outskirts of Berlin so we usually had time to make for the air raid shelter after the sirens wailed out their warning. But one day the sirens sounded and we heard the aeroplanes approaching before we reached the shelters. The noise of the engines seemed much louder than usual. When the anti-aircraft guns opened up, the bursts of shells picked out line after line of advancing planes. I knew the outlines of many of our bombers but I could not identify these planes. They were huge and far bigger than any that I had ever seen. They made no attempt at evasion, maintaining the same flight path and keeping a solid formation. They just kept coming on like a flock of geese except that they did not disperse when the shells exploded around them.

Many planes from the first wave were hit, bursting into flames and descending at an ever increasing speed and noise until they met their end in an almighty explosion. I had watched our planes plummeting from the sky like this during the Battle of Britain. I knew that many of the RAF pilots then were young and inexperienced. Some of the Spitfires had plummeted in a ball of fire and hit the ground with a massive explosion that cremated the young pilots in an instant. My heart had bled for them then, and now, four years later, I had the same feelings as I watched the shells from the Anti-aircraft guns hitting the bombers.

Although they were dropping bombs that might blow me to smithereens, I felt for these lads spiralling to their deaths, so many broken hearts at home. The same applied, of course, to the recipients of the bombs down below. The individual planes did not seem to select specific targets. The bombs of the first wave exploded almost simultaneously over a wide area and I certainly had the feeling that their bombs were devastating whole areas, not just specific targets.

As they came nearer and nearer we suddenly realised that the Daimler Benz factory might be a target. Everybody rushed for the air raid shelter because the camp would be well within the target area. It could be wiped out. We heard next day on the BBC news that the huge bombers were the Flying Fortresses of the USA Air Force. We all wanted to wish them luck - except on the occasions when we were in the target area.

I have mentioned the terrifying effect that the sirens of the "Dive Bomber" on Crete had as the plane dived. The effect of the bombing by the Flying Fortresses was much worse because of the noise created by the explosion of the sheer mass of bombs. Even when the explosion was a distance away, the blast shook the walls and roof of the air raid shelter to the point of collapse. The Daimler Benz factory was obviously a target because the noise of the explosions became deafening. Even if you covered your ears, you felt that they would burst any minute. The ground was shaking as though an earthquake was starting.

A few of the men began to moan as if they could not stand any more and the smell of excrement revealed that they were near to cracking up. It really was terrifying. If you had to walk the mile to the

Daimler Benz factory, it would seem a long distance. To the men crouching down in the shelter, a mile away from the factory being bombed was no distance at all. It felt as though the bombs were dropping just outside the camp perimeter. I crouched down, covered my ears and hoped that my luck in surviving this far would continue. If I were a cat, I would by now be running out of lives. It seemed an eternity until the bombing stopped. There was the most tremendous stampede for the toilets and once again I realised the major weakness of the mighty male of the species, the bowels.

When I emerged from the shelter, I expected the camp to be decimated. Dense smoke and flames were rising all around us and also away towards the factory. The scene in the direction of the Daimler Benz Factory looked as though German planes would be short of an engine for a long time. The camp huts were covered in shrapnel and the ground was littered with the silvery coloured material that was supposed to blank out the direction finders of the Anti-Aircraft guns.

Miraculously the camp was undamaged. A big sigh of relief went up and we were so thankful it was over, even if it was only for a short spell. We made for our huts, hoping for a good night's sleep. Maybe it was over now, but tomorrow was another day.

Tomorrow was indeed another day but we had not reckoned on the night that preceded it. I believe that this was the beginning of the final destruction of Berlin. I lay down in bed that night and fell sound asleep. It felt as though my eyelids had scarcely closed when I was awakened by that sound that made the nerves tingle, the wailing of the sirens. Not the Flying Fortresses back already, I thought?

It was not the American giants, it was a night raid by the RAF. I thought of my prayers in Crete for more planes. My prayers were being answered, but somewhat late and I was in the wrong place. As I crawled out of bed with bleary eyes, I could have cursed but only very briefly because the bombardments should help to shorten the war.

The RAF bombed all night but perhaps not with the same density as the Fortresses. The combined efforts of the Flying Fortresses by day and the RAF by night had a tremendous effect on us. My nerves were shattered and I lost sense of time so I could not remember how many days it lasted. If lack of sleep and shattered nerves made us fit for nothing, it must have been a hundred times worse for the civilians and soldiers who had to go out to work each day.

That series of attacks on Berlin went on with undiminished intensity day and night over a long period. Damaging the morale of the population could have been part of the objective. I am not making comments, critical or otherwise, on the morality of the bombing policy. I am merely writing about the relative effects on me, an individual who was subjected to the bombing by the different methods used in the two areas of war.

I mentioned that I had adopted the attitude of the First World War veterans: "If my name is on the bomb or bullet, there is nothing I can do". That stoical philosophy helps even if you can't prevent your stomach churning when bombs are dropping all around you and the building is shaking. Yet I must confess that a stoical philosophy was difficult to maintain at the height of the bombing.

Throughout the war a sense of humour always lightened the most despondent circumstances. That wee air raid shelter was the scene of many a laugh. One incident involved someone who should have been in the shelter. Seaman Johnson was one of the Genshagen real characters and the oldest resident in the camp. He was a sailor in the Merchant Navy and was taken into captivity when his ship sank.

I did not know his age but I placed him at 40+. The Merchant Navy was non-combative so strictly speaking he should not have been in a POW camp. He was always addressed as Seaman Johnson. I gathered that he had never been asked to work but someone must have decided he deserved a holiday. He wasn't in the best of health and suffered badly with stomach ulcers. He should have been home long before.

Today my elderly digestion rebels at certain rich foods. Nevertheless, when I am invited to a dinner that I know will drive my digestion up the wall, I cannot resist the temptation. I am reminded, therefore, of the occasion when I called on Marine Johnson and found him lying on his bed, groaning. I asked whether I should call for the medic. He said that he would be OK when The Bastard calmed down. He usually referred to his ulcer as The Bastard. It transpired that he had scoffed a whole tin of corned beef, a commodity that played havoc with his ulcer.

"Why on earth did you do that," I said, "You know it gives you hell." He answered with a twinkle in his eye: "I haven't touched corned beef for ages, so I decided to give The Bastard something to really groan about." What a character!

After a particularly heavy air raid, someone observed that Seaman Johnston was not in the shelter. There was a panic and feelings of guilt that only vanished when they found him sound asleep in his bed. True to character he had decided that he was fed up with trailing up to the air raid shelter night and day so he just went to bed and slept through an air raid that had everyone else shaking in their shoes.

Time was passing, and I was very concerned that John Brown had not recently mentioned the plan to escape to France. Admittedly he was often away. The heels of our boots had long ago been prepared to receive the documents and we certainly were ready to receive our orders. I was really geared up for this opportunity finally to achieve something worthwhile in this war. A success in this would compensate for all those "Almosts" and another disappointment this time would be the heart breaker.

I couldn't settle down to anything for thinking about this chance of a lifetime. With all this war activity, I felt that our big opportunity was fading away. I knew in my heart that the long delay with not a word to assure us could mean that the plan might be aborted.

Whatever power from above was guiding my fate in this war took a hand again because word came that the whole project was cancelled. The disappointment was all the greater because there were no explanations. Nobody contacted us. John Brown was still away and far too preoccupied with much more serious matters.

I was really down in the dumps – one more time when a decision entirely out of my control had a drastic affect on my immediate future. Another "Almost". I found a spot where I would not be seen, yes, I almost wept tears of frustration. Once more I had to shake myself out of a bout of self-pity. Nobody knows what fate has in store for one so I simply put my mind to the problems that lay ahead.

Goodbye Genshagen

The war finally caught up with Genshagen and the situation changed. No more parties arrived. In the developing war situation, it would have been ridiculous to expect any more. The staff had no function and I felt that we must soon be disbanded.

So it was not unexpected when, without warning, I was told to be ready to move. I had to say my sad goodbyes to my new friend, Benny. He was returning to the salt mines and I to the quarry. I was soon on a train bound, I assumed, for Praskovitz.

When I had passed through Berlin in the summer the extent of the damage had shaken me, now the city looked like a moonscape. Whole areas were laid to waste with scarcely an undamaged house. How much longer could the Germans hold out?

Homelessness must now be lowering the morale of a civilian population already badly affected by news of the Allies advancing into the Vaterland and by the sight of so many injured soldiers returning from the various Fronts. The advance of the Allies ever further into the Reich was creating a state of instability in Germany.

I sat in the train deliberating, both on my recent past at Genshagen and on my immediate future. My stay at Genshagen and my position on the staff there were fairly innocuous. The part proposed for me in the plan to escape to France with documents incriminating members of the British Free Corps was a different kettle of fish.

POW's from other camps had said to me that many were very suspicious that John Brown could be collaborating with the Germans.

I was still sure that John Brown was no collaborator. However, his knowledge of the members of the British Free Corps left a question mark in my mind about other activities in which he might be involved. If the Germans had reason to search Genshagen after it was closed, they might discover the documents that I had volunteered to take back to Britain. If they found anything to link the documents to Benny and me, our part in it might be classed as espionage. In that case, I would be a marked man.

On reflection that sounds daft because I was but a very small pawn, but you never know, they might decide that I was a budding James Bond. I decided that, if possible, I would keep a low profile about Genshagen until after the war when all might be revealed.

When we left the train and headed along the side of the river Elbe, I knew then that I was returning to Praskovitz. That was a relief but I was not out of the woods yet. I looked forward to meeting all my friends again but the prospect of another winter at the quarry face was not so attractive. Apart from the bitter cold, I was certain that my muscles, soft with weeks of inactivity, would rebel.

I was given a welcome on entering the camp and the lads were very interested to hear about Genshagen. I dwelt on its good points and was able to say truthfully that everything seemed to be open and above board. When they heard about the accommodation, the leisure activities and the visits to Berlin, they were quite envious and I felt a bit mean. They were not so jealous when they heard about the horrendous air raids.

The British Free Corps was not mentioned so it was apparently a non-starter as a subject for discussion. They were astounded that the camp was so close to target areas for Allied bombing, appreciating that lack of air raids was one of the few plus points of being a rural camp.

I had scarcely settled down when my concern about spending another winter at the quarry was dispelled, but only to be replaced by an even greater worry.

Chapter 10

Czechoslovakia

Stalag IVB - Coal Mine

I was pleased to be back in a rural area where I could keep a low profile, unfortunately not for long. One morning I was told to be ready to move. No explanations were offered.

I was very concerned. Were my worst fears about to be confirmed? When we were in the train, I asked the escort where we were going but he was not communicative and that made me more apprehensive. We finally pulled up at the entrance to a POW camp.

It was much bigger than Praskovitz but it was too small for the usual Stalag. I assumed that it was a working camp and I was relieved because my main concern was that interrogation might be the reason for my move. A working camp would hardly be the place for an interrogation.

When I was settled in, my new colleagues asked me the usual questions. I said truthfully that I had been working in a quarry at a working camp called Praskovitz on the River Elbe. I was determined to be a nonentity and I decided not to tell the story of Genshagen until I knew the lie of the land.

I asked about the work. They said that I would find it very different from a quarry and I could not believe my ears when I heard that it was a coalmine. First a quarry, at the top of a mountain with sub zero temperatures in winter, now the other extreme, down in the heat of the bowels of the earth, away from fresh air and sunshine.

I thought, well a coalmine was at least one way of avoiding the freezing weather. Somebody up there either has never seen a coal mine or has a wicked sense of humour. Maybe the same power that arranged for my friend, Benny, a coal miner in civilian life, to work as POW down a Silesian salt mine.

The big question had still not been answered. Why had I been sent here and why had nobody spoken to me about the change? As long as I was a nonentity, I was not desperately anxious to know the reason for my move.

A completely new experience awaited me on the morrow. I was not too enamoured at the thought that in the short days of winter I would be going down the mine in the dark and coming back up in the dark. That could mean that from one week to the next I would only see daylight at the weekend. By the time that the lighter nights came I would be as "peelie wally" as the proverbial china "Wally Dug".

My big hope was that the war would end soon and give me a blessed release. Meantime, I would have to soldier on for these last few months and make the best of it.

Despite these gloomy thoughts, I was quite interested to find out whether a miner's job was as black as it was painted. Next day I walked into the lift at the pithead and waited for the descent into the bowels of the earth. I got my first surprise. It did not descend gently like a commercial lift, nice and slowly so as not to upset the customers. It plummeted down as though the rope had parted company with it. I thought that I had left my stomach at the surface but luckily it caught up with me before I arrived at the bottom.

My next surprise was the wide cross section of men from European countries that assembled at the bottom of the shaft. At Praskovitz all the POW's were British, apart from the Cypriots, and civilians were few and far between. In the mine there were many more civilian workers than POW's. Some were Germans, skilled workers exempt from war service, and the usual proliferation of slave labour from the occupied countries.

I was allocated to work as labourer to a Pole and a Czech. They must have drawn the short straw. They were probably well acquainted with POW assistants and had no real expectation of their workload being lightened in any way.

I was surprised at the size of the place and the long distances to get to the coalface. We progressed up one of the branch lines until we came to what I thought was a dead end. It wasn't. The tunnel continued but the height dropped to about 4 to 5 feet. For a beginner, the pit props supporting the sides of the tunnel seemed ominously short and small. The whole set-up looked most insecure and, if you were claustrophobic, it would be quite terrifying.

We had to bend double until we entered a large circular chamber with a high roof. This was the coalface. The miners started to dig out the coal but to my relief, I was not given a pick. My task was to push the loaded wagon out of the way and replace it with an empty one. The loaded wagon was hooked on to an overhead moving cable and it trundled away to the main shaft, not an intellectually demanding task. My first day down the mine confirmed me in my opinion that spending the whole day underground was not attractive and, of course, nipping up to the surface for breath of air was out of the question, a thought that only a rookie like me would entertain.

Neither of my workmates spoke fluent English. The Pole had a smattering of English and the Czech had an equal smattering of German. We could just about make ourselves understood, even if the conversation was not exactly scintillating. I was able to extract a little information. I learned that we were near the town of Pilsen. We made up for the deficiencies with miming and body language and it was amazing how much we could communicate. At the end of the first day, I was glad to walk out of the pithead and breathe in the clean fresh air.

On the way to the shower, I glanced in a mirror and almost collapsed with shock. My face was black and not just ordinary black but a grimy, patchy and all over black with grey edges, like a badly made up singer in a "Black and White Minstrel Show"*. I stood under

[* These shows, which would nowadays be considered very non-politically correct, were very popular on British television in the late 50s and early 60s. Half the cast were "white", while the other half made up as "black" singers.]

the shower for ages. On the way out, I looked in the mirror but this time I was looking at my face. Despite being under the shower for ages, I still had coal dust in my ear lobes. No wonder I thought that they all looked peelie wallie. What would I be like in a week or a month?

A few weeks after my arrival, I noticed a perceptible increase in the number of POW's who accepted me and took me into their company. When a newcomer arrived in the mine, he was treated with caution at first because the Germans were guilty of introducing fifth columnists into camps, especially if they had any suspicions about matters such as sabotage. A single newcomer would be watched particularly carefully for a while until it was agreed that he should be accepted.

Jan, my Polish fellow worker, and I became friends. I knew that Jan had accepted me when he began to tell me about his background and his terrible experiences at the hands of the Germans. He told me about life in Poland after the German occupation. He could have been describing a scene in a horror film but I doubt whether a writer could have imagined such scenes.

Apparently the Germans showed an inhumanity to the Poles that I thought had no place in this day and age. I was sickened by Jan's description. Murder, pillage and rape devastated the whole population. Jan was wrenched from his home and from his family, with little hope of ever seeing them again. Indeed he did not know whether they were still alive. Jan was one of thousands who were taken into Germany to work in the mines or other forms of hard labour.

I thought that my lot was hard but the Poles were treated literally like slaves. Despite all these deprivations, Jan thought of himself as one of the lucky ones –just to be still alive. Many of his friends and family might by now have been rounded up and taken away to God knows where.

He was puzzled as to why he had not "disappeared" like the rest of his family, but he did not ask questions. He probably only escaped this fate because the Germans were desperate for slave labour to release

Jan Marmulwier, Author's Polish friend and fellow coalminer. On the right is the inscription on the back of his photo

more men for the war against Russia. He gave the impression that to survive he must make himself inconspicuous and keep well away from controversial situations. He actually preferred being down the mine because he had less chance of an unprovoked encounter with some fanatical Nazi. He said that his country was grateful to the British soldiers who came to the aid of Poland in 1939. Knowing that I was not entitled to bask in such praise, I tried to look suitably bashful.

Talking of sabotage, I was interested to hear about some of the ploys that the POW's had dreamt up to disrupt work without being detected. The Germans classed it as sabotage but the POW's looked on it as fair game, ie it wasn't sabotage in the sense of blowing up the mine.

The fact that the POW's let me in on their sabotaging secrets pleased me because I knew that I was really accepted. It sounds a bit like signing the thief's charter but we were, after all, prisoners.

They told me about one of their favourite ploys to gain a short respite from the daily grind. They joined two electrical wires that were attached to the roof and ran the length of all the railway lines. If they were brought into contact with one another, a bell rang at the pit-head and wagons on that stretch halted until the reason for ringing the bell was discovered, a derailed wagon, for example. It took a while for the control team to reach the sector in which the signal was situated. In a genuine warning, the fault might be cleared before the person from control arrived in the sector but the perpetrators had it well worked out how long it took for the control to arrive. In the meantime they could have a snooze and untie the wires before he came. I appreciated that ploy.

It reminded me of a trick we played as kids on a grumpy neighbour in our tenement in Glasgow. She was not a bit fond of children and thought that kids should be seen and not heard. If the youngsters started to play a game of football in the street she would run to the Police station to tell the local Bobby. In those days it was a criminal offence but the local Bobby usually ignored it.

The boys were fed up to the teeth with her meanness to children so they devised a plan. They tied a stone to a piece of string, fastened it with a pin on to her window. They pulled the string so that the stone banged the window. Then they dropped a milk bottle on the ground so that the glass scattered under the window and they ducked out of sight.

The lady came out, saw the glass on the pavement and ran off to the police station – no phones in working class tenements in those days. The boys knew that in this case he would have to take action because a misdemeanour was being reported so they rushed back, cleaned up the glass and hid.

When the policeman and the lady appeared, the astonishment on her face and the efforts of the policeman not to burst out laughing was ample reward for their ingenuity. It was a one-off trick. The sabotage in the mine brought back pleasant memories of home but the consequences of being caught committing sabotage down the mine would be drastically different, no smothered laughter from the mine police.

This camp had a wireless so news of the war situation was circulated regularly. Just before the end of the year, two items of interest came through, one good and one not so good. The first was that the Germans had made a counter attack on the Ardennes on the Western Front. Was it possible that the Allies could be beaten back? That news was a real blow to us. We were thinking of the war ending in a month or two. Hope springs eternal. The interest for me was that the Ardennes was in the area where we had planned to get through the lines. I wondered whether a build up of forces in the area in preparation for the German advance was perhaps the reason why the plan was aborted.

The good news was that the Russians had taken the city of Budapest. The reservation about that was the worry that the Russians would arrive before the Western Allies.

The cosmopolitan nature of the camp gave me a lot of interest and also much pleasure. Many European countries were represented. Many prisoners had been in Germany since the beginning of the war. Most, like me, could speak enough German to carry out a reasonable conversation. We talked a lot about the life in our respective countries.

I thought I had a reasonable knowledge of home and foreign affairs. But conversations with my new colleagues gave me a very different slant to many aspects of their countries. In return, they expressed surprise at some of the false British conceptions of their countries.

The pit face of a mine must have been the most unique venue for a working class debating society. It made up for the boring nature of the job and we could speak with freedom because the guards never came down the mine. If any of the workers were known to be collaborators or even were known to have leanings toward the Nazi philosophy, they were well watched. You could understand why I was watched so carefully when I arrived with no known background.

I was delighted when one of the Russians recited a poem by Rabbie Burns. Burns was considered an icon of socialism in Russia and his poems were on the curriculum of many schools. He recited it in Russian, so I only knew that he was reciting Rabbie because he told me. I clapped enthusiastically but for all I knew he could have been saying that Churchill was a silly old capitalist.

A while back we were optimistically saying "Home for Christmas", but the days and months were passing and, although the reports of the advances were good, the Germans were putting up a solid resistance.

Last Christmas we had had Red Cross parcels, allowing for a very reasonable meal. This year the food was generally back to the standard of 1941. In fact it was considerably worse and, with the Reich encircled and battles raging on all fronts, it was to be expected that parcels would have no priority.

The cook at the camp was French and he announced that he would manage somehow to have at least a good main course for Christmas. It was more than good, it was excellent. Chicken cooked in a beautiful sauce. I remember it so well because food right up to the end of the war was very scarce.

Some time after Christmas, the absence of the camp cats was noted and the cook was forced to confess to a group of cat lovers that the cats had contributed to the Christmas dinner. They made a great fuss which the cook and his French compatriots could not understand. To hear the comments, you would think that a heinous crime had been committed.

It is amazing how tastes in different cultures vary so widely. It was the conservative, with a small 'c', British who were mainly upset. They felt quite queasy at the thought. The hunger that I had endured in the past four years had made my tastes very catholic and I was surprised at the reaction because I thought that hunger would have overcome their culinary prejudices.

Since at least the beginning of the War the practice of eating dogs had been accepted in Germany. I had no inhibitions about eating and enjoying the wee hedgehogs cooked by my Cypriot friends. If I had known that it was cat I might have had reservations about eating it. The old saying is true: "Hunger is the best sauce" and I did enjoy that lovely meal.

Another Hogmanay passed and it was as quiet as Aberdeen on a Flag Day. A number of people made optimistic resolutions on the assumption that the New Year would bring an end to the war, regretfully I did not have a wee dram to toast that resolution.

The latest news was that Warsaw had fallen and that the Russians had reached Silesia. The Eastern Front really was close. The news about the fall of Warsaw was followed by news of a conference between Churchill, Roosevelt and Stalin where an agreement had been reached on the lines of demarcation, a line at which the respective armies would halt once the Germans surrendered.

I don't suppose that was of any great interest to most people back home. It was of intense interest to my fellow miners from Poland and other eastern countries. They felt that being on the wrong side (the east) of that line could dramatically affect their future. They hated the Germans but they positively dreaded the thought of their countries being occupied by the Russians.

I had no real reason to think that British POW's on the wrong side of the demarcation line would not be returned to the Allied zone but the Russians were so unpredictable. Their views on capitalist countries and their reaction to Churchill's views on communism were well known. After Germany was defeated, the wartime alliance might disappear like "snaw aff a dyke." If that happened, the Russians might consider that thousands of American and British POW's could be useful cards to have in any negotiations. It was only speculation and it did not stop me being over the moon that the end of the war must be near.

My whole approach to my situation in captivity had changed. It was almost four years since Crete was surrendered. Four long years during which my life had reached it's lowest ebb. No matter how optimistic I tried to be, the situation was abysmal. Incarceration, semi-starvation, frustration seemed to be my lot for an indefinite and hopeless future.

I risk being boring when I refer so frequently to my strong feelings about incarceration, but these feelings constantly dominated my thoughts. My present environment in the coalmine was perhaps worse than the open air of the quarry. A real but not unexpected blow was the cessation of the Red Cross parcels at a time when rations for everybody in Germany reached a new low.

The immediate future was fraught with danger. Despite all that, I was mentally, if not physically, in good nick. The difference now was that the end of the war, freedom, home and family were all fixed firmly in my sights. I was perhaps impatient but I was sure that it was just a matter of time.

So buoyed by these thoughts was I that I kept going on about what I would do when we got home. I selfishly lost sight of the effect that the news would have on Jan, his fellow Poles and all those from the other occupied countries of Eastern Europe. Their homes were all East of Berlin. The news of the fall of Warsaw brought mixed feelings to them.

They were, of course, overjoyed that their capital city was no longer under the yoke of the Nazis. On the one hand they hoped that their families might now be free and they might see them all soon. On the other hand they were very pessimistic. Jan had spoken about the extermination of whole communities. They would all fear that their families might have been killed and their homes destroyed. I knew about the even greater fear that the Russians might be worse. I should not have forgotten how deep that fear ran. Their last hope of the Allies releasing them was gone. Their only hope, a forlorn one, was that they might be completely wrong in their assessment of the Russian's future actions.

Although I was still ecstatic about the marvellous prospects that the next few months might bring for me, I was devastated for all those in the mine with whom I had struck such an enlightening and fulfilling friendship. These friendships more than compensated for the subterranean environment that I disliked so much.

I still marvel at the discussions that took place in our mini-debating society during the breaks. It would be difficult to find a more unlikely conglomeration of participants. The intellectual quality could scarcely compare to Oxford or Cambridge, except in the enthusiasm and thirst for knowledge. Before the war I had never travelled abroad and my knowledge of the peoples of Europe and their cultures was limited to books or cinema films.

My first experience of people with a different culture was when the Cypriots came to the Praskovitz POW camp. It was not, of course, the same as visiting them in their home country but, nevertheless it was a marvellous experience and I learned so much about life in Cyprus. It taught me tolerance of other people's culture, their eating habits and other customs, many of which derived from the disciplines of their religion. In Praskovitz, I learned also to be far more tolerant of other people's idiosyncrasies and habits, habits that could irritate beyond belief after years of living in close proximity.

The discussions held by that little group in a wee corner of a Czechoslovakian coal mine widened my tolerance still further. The breadth of the discussions was obviously restricted by the language barrier but overcoming that problem was a revelation in itself.

More important than general and political matters was clarification and help on problems that had been bottled up because everyone had to be so careful about expressing grievances in public. I was there for only a matter of months but I left feeling that it was one of the most instructive and useful experiences of my POW time. Others felt the same and I was touched by some of the expressions of thanks.

My friend Jan gave me a photograph of himself with an inscription on the back "Ich nicht vergessen tu bist mein zehr gut Koleg". These are his words, not mine. It translates roughly "I do not forget that you are my good comrade". The spelling and grammar might be wrong but it showed that you can express your friendship and affection despite spelling and grammar not being 100% correct. I did appreciate his thoughts. None of our little group had the tremendous advantage of a University education but, if a POW camp could be called a University of Life, perhaps we could claim to have passed with honours in a four-year study of "Tolerance in Incarceration".

The days and weeks dragged on but everything except the war situation paled into insignificance. Even the level of production was apparently no longer concerning the managers of the mine. The guards and the German workers were in an increasing state of "angst" about the approaching Russians. The news that Dresden had been heavily bombed made us anxious as to whether any of our colleagues in Stalag IVB had been affected.

I had hoped at one time that I might be home for my birthday in April, just five years after I was called up to the Marines. The birthday passed and the Germans still had not surrendered. Then came the news that put all the Germans into a state of panic. The Russians had surrounded Berlin and, even more sensational, Hitler had committed suicide.

That act must have undermined even the most fanatic of the Nazis, and, surely, I thought, the war must end now? No fear, it still dragged on.

The Germans guarding the camp were bound to withdraw before the Russians appeared but the problem for us was whether there would be a reasonable gap between the two events and what sort of chaos would erupt in the nearby towns when they did withdraw?

I began to make a contingency plan to head West as soon as the guards vamoosed. I decided that all I could do meantime was to put aside some food in case I had to go to ground and decide whether to wear my uniform or the miner's clobber. The blighters made us go down the mine every day even though the work rate was minimal. It was maddening.

At last, one morning early in May, we could hear in the distance the sound of loud explosions that sounded like heavy artillery. Incredulously they still sent us down the mine that day. The chance of a reasonable gap between the German withdrawal and the Russian arrival was diminishing. If the camp was going to be shelled, we should stay down until it was over. Another good reason for not surfacing was the possibility that some Germans might decide to kill the POW's before they retreated.

Part 4

The End of the War in Europe

Chapter 11

The Russians Arrive

Free at Last

We sat at the pitface for a day that was like a year. No work was done at all. Finally, the sound we were waiting to hear rang out, shouts of: "The guards have gone, the guards have gone" came from the main tunnel and men ran like mad for the pithead.

There was some disorder around the lift but eventually I reached the pithead. The sight that greeted me shook me rigid. Standing at the gate was a huge Russian tank and excited POW's were talking to the crew. My first thought was: "Oh, God, the Russians are here first and all my contingency planning is up the creek," but the sight of the Russians chatting away to the lads chased that thought out of my mind.

This was it. This was the moment that I had dreamed about for years. It was not quite the scene that I had anticipated but it was the beginning of a new era of freedom. As it sunk in, I could at that moment have beaten all Olympic records for the high jump and, if a bottle of the hard stuff had been around, I might have drunk myself into a stupor. I was certainly emotionally drunk with joy and nothing that happened now could take away that glorious feeling.

I saw that the lads at the gates had drinks in their hand and they were making plenty noise but there was no panic, only the noise of laughter and merriment. The Russians were obviously friendly so I approached a smiling member of the crew who immediately offered me a drink. Champagne and glasses were not part of their kit but he balanced a large can on his shoulder and tipped a huge dram into a mug. It looked like petrol but it was my first introduction to vodka. He mimed that it should be swallowed without a pause. My innards had not been introduced to alcohol for many moons so I hoped that I would not shame the nation by collapsing in a heap. It was not as smooth as whisky but it went down quite well and I was soon feeling friends with the world.

Though I had been very anxious about the first encounter with the Russians it was quite a good introduction to freedom. The tank moved off but more importantly, there was no sign of the support infantry following in the rear of the tanks. I decided to get quickly back to my hut and make new plans for heading west to the Allied lines.

There was no disorder in the camp but there was no leadership either and I had the impression that people were reluctant to leave the security of the camp until the situation outside was known.

People were walking around aimlessly. A majority decided that it was better not to leave meantime even though the fighting in this area was now finished.

There were a number of unknown factors. How far had the Germans withdrawn and had they surrendered? Where was the demarcation line and had the Russian troops bypassed it to reach us? Was the resistance movement taking advantage of a vacuum in authority to wreak their revenge on collaborators? A large number of POW's moving in any of these situations might be at risk.

I decided that I would try to find out the state of affairs in the district to the West of the camp. A loner could wander about without being conspicuous. I knew that one of the miners lived somewhere to the West but I did not know whether it was a village or a small town. I had decided to be ready to get out fast if the need arose but I had never been outside the perimeter so a bit of reconnaissance would be useful.

We still did not know whether the war was officially over but I was free and there was nothing to stop me exploring the area around the camp. As I walked out into the open and past that accursed barbed wire fence, a surge of joy went through me. I was actually free. I could have danced my way down the street singing like Julie Andrews that the hills were alive with the sound of music.

In the circumstances, that would have been a bit conspicuous but I could not stop myself smiling and I gave the thumbs up sign as I passed people. That was more than a wee bit careless because I had not a clue who or what they were. Luckily they all waved back and I soon calmed down.

As I passed the gate of a cemetery, I heard the sound of small arms fire and I could see a number of civilians lined up alongside a pit. Facing them was a group of civilians and they had rifles. I was transfixed as I realised that it was a firing squad. They aimed and fired. The bodies fell forward into the pit. Without delay another group was marched to the side of the pit. I had no idea who was shooting or who was being shot. All of them wore civilian clothes so it was most likely a local resistance group holding a kangaroo court and administering rough justice to collaborators. I decided to depart the scene at a high rate of knots. I was on what seemed to be a main road and it led in a westerly direction so it would suit my purpose. I made my way back to the camp, whistling like a lark all the way. It wouldn't be long until I was whistling like a linnet on my way up Loch Long.

Rescued by the USA Army

I am sure that you have all experienced moments of real joy in your lives. I have had many, but I am now about to write about an experience that was so joyful that it still thrills me to re-live it.

After I came back from my reconnaissance trip, I began to feel very frustrated at my situation. I thought to myself: "Here I am, free at last and yet I am sitting around waiting for something to happen". I decided that I would wait until tomorrow morning for a decision to move out.

If no decision was made I would make for the Allied Line before the Russian occupation force arrived. I would go, preferably with someone to accompany me, but on my own if necessary. I would have no gear to encumbrance me. I had some food that I had put by and some Czech currency that I acquired for such a situation as this. I was ready to go next day.

My thoughts must have winged across the ether because the next morning pandemonium broke out. A large convoy of trucks drove into the camp and at first we thought it was the Russians. To our delight it was an American convoy from a Transport Group stationed at the demarcation line further west. They had heard that a whole camp of POW's was held up inside the Russian line. Allied troops were not supposed to cross the agreed line, but with typical American cussedness, they decided to make a dash over the line to find us and bring us back before the Russian troops arrived.

The drivers jumped down, lowered the tailboard and shouted that they had only minutes to spare so we ran around shouting and rounded up as many as we could, no packing for anything. The American sergeants yelled in the way they do when they want everybody to jump to it. "Go, Go, Go," they shouted.

The speed of evacuation shook even the Americans. A quick check to make sure that nobody was still dossing somewhere and then we were off. There must have been somebody left behind and I felt sorry. I was still haunted by the day in Crete when I was left behind. A lot of the drivers were coloured and they were so animated and obviously so delighted that they had found us, that they joked, sang songs and laughed all the way.

I was full of the joys of spring and I sang and laughed with them. They were driving like bats out of hell but I stood up at the back of the cab all the way. My eyes were sore and streaming with tears, not with emotion, but with the wind. I feasted them on the beautiful countryside racing past. This time it was not just because of its beauty but because it was racing past at high speed. I was not going to sit down and shelter because every moment was another moment to savour, another moment nearer to complete freedom.

I had often used the word "Joy" but never with the deep emotion

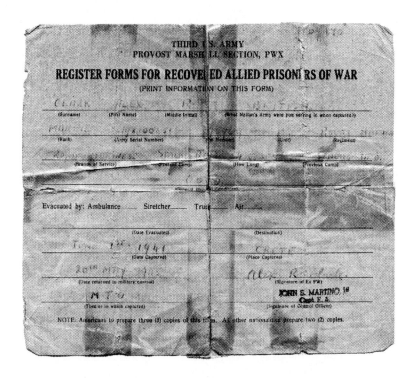

Registration Form for Recovered Allied Prisoner of War. My form noted that I was captured on the 1st June, 1941, and returned to military control on 20th May, 1945, only 11 days short of 4 years. I was amused that my Marine serial number, CHX100651, was now accompanied by that other number I had hoped I might never again be asked to recognise, my POW number, 95969. At least it was on a disk and not tattooed like on the poor souls in Belsen.

that swelled up inside me as that truck sped on its bumpy way. I was so elated that it was almost a spiritual experience.

When we arrived at the town of Pilsen, I was amazed at the number of people lining the streets. They were cheering as we passed. The convoy stopped for a moment and we asked the driver why the people were cheering. He said that word had got round that a large number of British POW's were being brought in from the Russian Sector and that they were showing their appreciation. Nobody had even recognised our existence for years. It felt so good.

I couldn't believe it but of course they would also be in a mood of exhilaration at the end of the German occupation. A Czech lady came forward, gave me a kiss and I floated away in ecstasy, feeling as if I was in heaven. She gave us bottles of the famous Pilsener, it tasted like nectar and then I knew that I was in heaven She was rewarded with a huge cheer.

The convoy made its way slowly until we reached their Post, The Provost Marshall Section, the equivalent, I was told, of the British Military Police. I was ushered into a room where an Officer said that he had a few questions to ask. For a few moments my heart stopped because Genshagen jumped into my mind but he only asked routine questions to ascertain that you were a genuine POW.

After a brief session to verify my authenticity, I was handed over to a GI who was to look after me. The older generation will know that a USA soldier was called a GI, an abbreviation for General Issue. I thought that "Hostilities Only" was a poor description of my status but "General Issue" sounded like a pair of underpants.

From that point on, I was thoroughly spoiled. I was subjected to the usual delousing although we were actually free of wee beasties. I hoped that this would be my last delousing and that the damned fleas and lice would decide to stay behind when I headed for Blighty. I was given clean clothes and then food.

As we had been so starved for the past few months I stood mesmerised at the sight of that canteen brimming over with food, food, glorious food. I sat looking at a huge plate of roast beef, vegetables and luscious gravy as though it was a Van Gogh painting. It seemed a shame to spoil the vision but I delved in with gusto. It was accompanied by a loaf of white bread fresh from the bakery with loads of creamy butter.

The GI's were not aware of the affect of such a plateful on stomachs unaccustomed for so long to such rich food. We should have been wary but the temptation was too much and we suffered badly but gladly. We were given a few lovely days in unaccustomed luxury to recover sufficiently to resume our journey home.

Every aspect of that journey ranks as one of the most memorable and enjoyable. The transport accommodation would have tourists today clamouring for a refund. To me it was heavenly and I was so grateful to the Americans providing us with such a magnificent welcome in our first experience of freedom for years.

Although I was anxious to see home again, I was quite relaxed. I had not realised the tremendous pressure of the last few months. The tension had now dropped away and I was satiated with the utter enjoyment of the environment. The rescue and the escape from the coalmine before the Russians arrived could be classed as the one important occasion when the "Almost Syndrome" did not strike. On the other hand many POW's who were in areas taken over by the Russians were transported to Russia and held there for a long time before eventually being sent home. My heart bled for them. They must have gone through mental torture.

The Royal Marines

The call came for the last stage of our journey. We were to be flown back to Blighty. On arrival at the airport we saw our plane sitting on the tarmac, a Lancaster bomber. When we entered the plane I thought how quickly things change. Not long ago this Lancaster might have been dropping bombs around Genshagen POW camp. Now it was on a mission much closer to my heart, taking me home.

The pilot was very attentive and asked me whether I would like to sit in the rear-gunner's cockpit at the back of the plane. "A really super view" he said. The plane was so big that I thought that everywhere would have plenty of space to walk about but I had to crawl along the fuselage to get to the rear gunner's cockpit, even crawling along to reach the coalface down the mine was no worse.

Cockpit was an appropriate description of the rear gunner's post because it was quite a step down to it and it was very cramped. I could picture how it must have felt when a Messerschmitt was coming up from the rear with all guns blazing. If, for any reason, he had to get out, it must have been a hazardous task. The cockpit could swivel round as the machine gun was turned. In my case it was only to look at the marvellous and kaleidoscopic view. I would have changed my mind about that if there had been another Messerschmitt on my tail - twice was quite enough for me!

The pilot came on the intercom to tell me that we were approaching the English Channel and the White Cliffs of Dover would come into view in a minute. He told me to switch on the intercom and I would have some nice music for my return to England.

I cannot remember the name of the orchestra but Max Jaffa at the Palm Court comes to mind. I felt like a VIP and I was so appreciative of the kind treatment that I had received since I left my last POW camp. It was such a dramatic change that you hoped you would not wake up to find it was all a dream.

In no time we were crossing the White Cliffs of Dover, the green fields of Kent and then coming in to land. The magic moment that I had dreamt of for so long was nigh, the moment that I would step on to the soil of the homeland.

When the plane stopped, the gangway was lowered and a number of people hurried towards us. I was not expecting a welcoming party but after the welcome the Americans gave us, nothing would have surprised me. The three Armed Forces were represented. An ambulance was standing by and a number of nurses came forward. I thought that I must have missed casualties boarding the plane but there were none.

An NCO told all Army personnel to fall in beside him. Nurses came forward and escorted them to a hanger that seemed to be laid out with refreshments.

A Royal Marine Sergeant approached and called out for any Royal

Marines to follow him. My uniform was a mixture like a bag of liquorice all-sorts. I could see that the Sergeant was not too enamoured either of my uniform or by my distinctly skeletal appearance. I did not look like a model Royal Marine.

For us there was no welcoming party, no refreshments and nurses were conspicuous by their absence. I was surprised and wondered what the Sergeant would have done if I had been unable to fend for myself. He asked me a few questions to ascertain my home base before I went abroad. As I was in Kent, I expected to be taken to Chatham, my home base just up the road but when I told him that my last posting had been Portsmouth, he said that I would be sent there.

He wrote for a moment, handed me a travel voucher and told me to report to the Marine barracks at Portsmouth. I was flabbergasted – no nurses, no refreshments, no money. I was back in the Marines so I did not argue. It did go through my mind that perhaps POW's were perhaps "infra dig" in the Marines but then I thought, surely not. He drove me to the station and left me there.

To say that I was taken aback would be more than an under-statement. Perhaps I was not thinking clearly after years of being incarcerated. Well, I had longed for freedom, had I not?

I sat in a corner of the compartment feeling very conspicuous in my continental uniform. I cannot remember which armies contributed to make it up. I think it was the USA and France. I had to change trains in London. I was peckish and thirsty but I had no British money. A Military Policeman was suspicious of my outfit and stopped me. He could scarcely believe my tale but he gave me money for refreshment.

When I arrived at Pompey, [Portsmouth to you], I had to walk to the barracks. I recalled the first time that I approached a Royal Marine barracks when I joined the Marines at Chatham away back in 1940. The guard looked down his nose at me then and I looked forward to the reaction of the guard at the gates of the barracks in Portsmouth when this apparition walked up.

The Marine guard was motionless when I approached the barrack gates. I can't remember whether he said the formal "Halt, who goes there." I would not have been surprised if he had said: "Who are you, what planet are you from and where the hell do you think you are going?" With his Marine cap in the normal position, he looked down his nose at me from a great height.

Disdain was his first emotion. Utter disbelief was his second, when I replied that I was reporting for duty and showed him my transport pass. He looked me up and down, his nose curling up almost to the brim of his cap. I was beginning to enjoy myself for the first time since I landed in Britain. He gave a thunderous shout for the Sergeant of the Guard who came charging out in response to see what provoked a shout like that. I stood motionless to attention as if I had the full Blues uniform. I had not stood like that for years, straight back, shoulders back, chin in and arms straight with the thumbs down the seams. I was a perfect Marine except that my uniform looked like it belonged to somebody out of a pantomime.

The guard explained the position and I was bundled at high speed into the guardroom out of sight of the public. Well, well, there was no doubt that I was back in the Marines. Sitting in the guardhouse with memories of my hiccups in training gave me a distinct feeling of "déjà vu".

My sojourn at Portsmouth was brief. I was given a quick check to make sure that I was not lousy - in the physical not the metaphorical sense. I was given a complete outfit and at last some food and drink. The next day the Doctor examined me and told me that I was suffering from a degree of malnutrition but that I would soon recover with a good diet although there might be complications later in life.

The Doctor, appreciating that I would be anxious to get away home on leave, advised me of the procedure with returning POW's. He said that if I had any ailment to report that might require examination I would be referred to the hospital and there could be a delay. If I had nothing to report, I could collect my pass and get off home immediately.

216

That was the quickest decision that I had made in years. I was pronounced medically OK and I was on the train in no time and away home. The period abroad, including the POW stint, counted as Foreign Service so I was entitled to a very long leave. I looked forward to a relaxing holiday.

I was looking forward to meeting my Mum and Dad again but I had a very strange feeling. I had been away so long and been through so much that, unbelievably, I felt something akin to apprehension. I managed to make a real mess of my arrival. I thought that it would be a nice surprise to take a tram from the station and see the old sights, then a short walk to my home street, a knock on the door and wait to enjoy the look on their faces.

I was a bit surprised to see the street festooned with bunting. It couldn't still be D-Day celebrations. Unwittingly I had made an absolute muck up of their homecoming celebration because it did not dawn on me that they would treat my homecoming as an event. My arrival in Britain and my reception by the Marines had made me feel that being a POW was something about which you kept quiet.

I felt so guilty at spoiling their day especially when the neighbours came round to present me with a wallet full of notes. I was very touched and I felt that at last I was really home.

Four years was an eternity in a POW camp but not much had changed at home except that all the 16 year old teenagers were in the Forces and most of the 12 year old kids were now working. I knew that I had undergone such big changes that adjusting to young people at home might prove difficult.

I had left home when I was only months out of my teens myself. In some ways I was still a "teenager" because I had not lived as a civilian through those formative years between 20 and 25. In my absence I had missed many social developments and I was naive. In other ways I was much older than 25 because the experiences I had undergone had aged me, at least psychologically, much more than I realised. A difficult period of adjustment faced me.

I was obviously going to find it difficult to fit in with those of my age group who had not undergone the ravages of war but had developed socially.

I was still too soon out of the POW life to cope with this problem so I went to the hills a lot. The hymn: "I to the hills will lift mine eyes from whence doth come mine aid", conveys a religious belief but the concept applied to me at that stage of my life. I headed for the hills on my trusty old bike, along the banks of the Clyde to Helensburgh and up Loch Fyne to Arrochar. I looked up at the Cobbler with the humpy peak that gave it its name.

I climbed up as far as my legs, weakened by malnutrition, would take me. A magnificent view came into sight, the memories of which had sustained me so often in prison camp when I had lain in bed and conjured up this view, blotting out the barbed wire at the windows.

Now I sat for hours, just soaking in the beauty of the scenery, the peace and quiet of the surroundings. This peace and quiet washed over me like a balm. The feeling above all that stirred my emotions was that I was FREE. FREEDOM was all around me.

How does one express these feelings after years in a POW camp? Of what it was to me to see the Scottish Mountains fill every horizon? I could now leave when I wanted, stay if I wanted, go north, south, east or west.

I still remembered sitting at the top of these mountains before the war and I had appreciated the views then. But real appreciation of freedom only really comes when you know what it is to have lost it. The memory of that symbol of incarceration may live with me forever but at least the sight of barbed wire at the windows will never greet me again every morning.

I thought long and deep during this long leave. I so enjoyed renewing and strengthening my love for my parents, family and friends. But I was ready to go back and do whatever was necessary until the end of the war with Japan.

After my leave, I was posted to my home depot of Chatham. So far there had been no indication that anyone or any group had considered the problem of POW's returning to active service.

I was aware that, although the period at home refreshed me and made me willing to have a go at regaining some of my previous fitness, I was not in a physical condition to undergo strenuous training. It takes time for the body to recover from long periods of malnutrition. Indeed the doctor who examined me at Portsmouth may not have done me any favours by letting me go on leave without officially recording the condition brought about by the four years as a POW.

Today there are experts on the subject but nobody seemed to have made a study of these conditions in 1945. I was put back immediately into full training.

There were two aspects to the training in 1945 that differed to that in 1940. The first was physical, the second technical. I had to start at the beginning again.

Radar was now commonplace and the Radio Detection Finder system for Anti-Aircraft guns was old hat. Most people that I spoke to gave me the impression that they now placed it somewhere around the bow and arrow era. The same applied to the technical level of small arms. The Lee Enfield was now in the museum where it belonged.

The Sergeant handed me a hand grenade and asked me to prime it but it was plastic with a handle and I had not a clue what to do with it. The hand grenade that I trained on was the 1914 version, the same vintage as the Lee Enfield, made of heavy metal, shaped like a pineapple and with a little ring that you used to pull out the pin. You counted to ten and threw it and, with a bit of luck, it did not explode until a few seconds after it landed. If you were a bad counter, you were not given a bollicking, a telegram was sent to your family.

The Sergeant was not all that long in the tooth and probably didn't realise the extent of the changes since the War began. He soon realised that Commando type training was beyond our physical capabilities. To my delight he raised the matter and to my greater delight the response was that I was to report to the Education Officer. He asked me to choose any subject that would fit me for a civilian job so I chose to study for the Civil Service Entrance examinations for entry to the Executive and Customs Officer Grades (five years after the cancelled exams in 1939).

My War is Over

My brain was in reasonable order but I could not apply myself to my studies. I was still at the stage of enjoying all the activities now freely available to me. The news that the Japanese had surrendered after the atomic bomb was dropped on Hiroshima meant that at last the war, in all areas, was over.

It was not long before an Officer walked into the room where I was studying and broke the marvellous news to the ex-POW's that orders to demobilise them had been announced. I knew that it would not be received kindly if I jumped through the roof so I refrained but I was soon out of that room like a flash.

In no time I was collecting my Austin Reed demob outfit. I was given a discharge certificate and a report of my annual performance over the five years. That report was a real shock. It confirmed my suspicion that the Marines did not want to recognise the existence of a Marine who had been a POW. The first year of my service was marked V.G. but the next 4 years were blank. That would take some explaining if I used it as a reference!

Although I had my civilian outfit, I still had to wear my uniform until I was clear of the barracks. Knowing that the Sergeant of the Guard would not allow me out of that gate unless I was 100% properly dressed, I paid particular attention to my appearance. I was just about to make my last step in the barracks when the Sergeant shouted "Halt."

He asked me how long I had been in the Marines. He knew damn well that I was an ex-POW but I responded properly in a loud voice: "Five years, Sergeant." "You should be wearing War Service and Long

Service medals, you are improperly dressed," That struck me as the ultimate irony for a Marine involved in the Battle of Crete. Many people had questioned why there had not been some recognition of that battle. I had no aspirations to wear medals. I was classified as "Hostilities Only".

I was ever so happy to be a civilian again but here I was being turned back at the last moment for the sake of a medal for just being in the war. I could have been peeling tatties for five years and been awarded those medals. I picked up the cloth version of the medals and had them sown on my uniform. Give the Sergeant his due, when we passed out this time, he had a broad grin on his face as he wished us a safe passage. His grin said it all. The Marines had the last laugh.

Numerous thoughts assailed me as I walked slowly down the street to Chatham railway station, that street of many weary route marches in 1941.

In my mind's eye I could see my old squad marching up to the barracks with their arms swinging shoulder high. The Sergeant would be shouting to them to bang those boots on the ground and put that infantry lot out of their stride.

I was not saddened by the ending of my war. I felt no bitterness. I had learned a hard lesson in tolerance and was just so thankful that I was free, safe and heading for home.

I looked back up to the barracks gates and pondered for a moment, I wondered where the lads in that squad were now. I felt gratitude that I had been successful in one of my main objectives for the War, just to survive it.

I also felt great sadness when I pictured the faces of some of those comrades with whom I had been through so much in Crete. I had survived. I was home. They would never leave Crete or Tobruck.

Conclusion

I hope I have achieved one of my main objectives in telling this story of my experiences in the Second World War. I tried to tell the story exactly as it happened to me at the time. I avoided, wherever possible, references to a post-war historical analysis of events or explanations as to why certain military strategies were followed.

However, now that my story is told I am taking the liberty of quoting many things that I have learned since the end of the war and which had a bearing on the events in which I was involved. I have added a number of Appendices that answer questions about so many of the actions in which I was involved, actions that I simply just could not fathom at the time.

Appendix A

The Amazing Story of John Brown D.C.M.

I never met up again with John Brown, the Senior NCO in charge of the Genshagen camp in Berlin. It was only after the war that I learned from the national newspapers about his work as a spy for MI6. He was a prime witness in the trial of William Joyce, the traitor better known as Lord Haw Haw.

After the war he wrote a book about the part he had played throughout the war which finally led to Joyce, and all those involved in the British Free Corps, coming to trial. Throughout the whole war John Brown had been suspected by the POW's in the Stalags of Lamsdorf and Blechhammer of sympathising with the Nazi regime. His name was linked with the British Free Corps. His leadership of the so-called Holiday Camp of Genshagen was considered a further example of collaboration with the Germans.

Nothing could have been further from the truth. John had been working for MI6 from the time that he became a POW. He deliberately created the impression that he was sympathetic to the Nazi regime as a ploy to gain the Germans' confidence and obtain information valuable to British Intelligence.

It was amazing that, for the duration of the war, John was able to lead a double life without the Germans discovering his true identity. More amazing than that was his achievement in fooling his fellow POW's for over four years. POW's lived an introspective existence and had so little privacy that the only safe secrets were those in your mind - and even those were at risk if you talked in your sleep. Thus, it was miraculous that only a few trusted friends knew about John's activities. Those who branded him a sympathiser or traitor never found out the truth until after the war

As I wrote in the Chapters about Genshagen and the British Free Corps, I knew nothing of the rumours sweeping through Lamsdorf and Blechhammer when I arrived at Genshagen. My only knowledge of the British Free Corps was the pamphlet distributed throughout British POW camps. Prior to my arrival at Genshagen, I had no knowledge of John Brown.

The invitation to send someone to Genshagen had aroused the curiosity of all at Praskovitz working camp. I was asked to find out as much as I could to satisfy that curiosity. For example, why did the Germans, who for years had treated POW's as slaves in hard labour camps at quarries, coal and salt mines, suddenly decide to give some of them a holiday in Genshagen? I agreed to go there but to keep my eyes open for anything suspicious that would justify this sudden change of heart.

Coming from a small and remote working camp, I could be considered a rustic in the POW politics of the large Stalags. As I knew nothing of the rumours circulating elsewhere, it was not surprising that I should see nothing suspicious in the first few weeks.

John Brown was a Senior NCO, a QM in the Royal Artillery, but he was not the epitome of the raucous and aggressive types who often held that rank. He was a gentleman in every sense. He was friendly, sincere, helpful, understanding and very willing to listen. He made excellent use of his ability to listen - an invaluable facility in his difficult task as a spy.

In Chapter 8 (Genshagen), I recounted how John asked Benny McLaughlin and me to take on the task of couriers to take information back to Britain about the leaders and members of the British Free Corps. The documents were to be miniaturised and would have been placed in the heel of our boots. A dissident German Officer whom John trusted would escort us to the Front Line in France and he would either lead us through to a British Army position or show us where we could break through unobserved. We placed our trust, and our lives, in John's trust of that German Officer, a big factor in our decision to accept that task. That was the first time that I had heard the British Free Corps mentioned so I had reason to pause and think. Was Genshagen a link with the British Free Corps? John said that he had managed to obtain the information. He was obviously not in a position to tell me any more. Benny and I talked it over for a long time. The attraction of an organised escape with the motivation of taking very important information back to Britain was powerful, an opportunity that might only arise once in a blue moon. For me it would compensate for many of the disappointments that had been my miserable lot in this war. We decided to go for it. The disappointment to Benny and me when the plan had to be abandoned was hard to bear.

When I heard of John's death in 1964, I was very sad that he did not have a longer time to enjoy a life of freedom after his years 'in durance vile'. John chose the words as the title of a book published posthumously. I acknowledge borrowing the phrase, 'in durance vile' for the heading of Part 3 in this book that relates to the POW period of my life. I am sure that he would not have objected to my using it. It is a succinct phrase that sums up all that he and I felt about incarceration.

The book was published in 1981 but I only discovered it recently. I did not put it down until I had read the last page. I have still not quite recovered from the impact of reading his account of his exploits as a spy during his period as a POW. In my relations with John at Genshagen, I was certain that he must have had contacts to be able to collect such secret information. The idea that he was a spy had never crossed my mind.

He handled the most dangerous situations with aplomb, calmness and a presence of mind that was amazing. I was stunned to find out he had been working for MI6 because I knew him only for the short time at Genshagen and had admired him as a gentle person who made time to listen to anyone who sought his advice. He gave encouragement to the lads whom he felt deserved a break from years of hard labour under the German jackboot. He did all this in his quiet unassuming way that, to me, was the antithesis of my concept of a hardened spy living in a constant state of tension and in fear of being detected.

Every new POW or German soldier who came to the camp was a potential threat to him. A greater threat was the possibility that some German officials, jealous of his influence in high circles, might obtain information to discredit him. When I think back, he must have studied Benny and me very closely before he chose us to act as couriers. We were prepared to take a big risk but that was nothing compared with what would have happened to him if the plan had failed and his role as a spy discovered.

John recorded examples of the kind of stressful situations that he had to face regularly. It demonstrated his sharpness and ability to deal with dangerous situations, where a split second's lack of concentration could mean the difference between life and death. Germans who mistrusted his supposed sympathy for the Nazi regime kept creating situations to catch him out. For example, he was taken into Berlin to meet someone whose identity was not revealed. Another POW was also waiting in the room for the person they were to meet. This POW had a German mother who was still in Germany and the Germans were trying to put pressure on him by inferring that, if he didn't co-operate, his mother might suffer. John knew this and decided that he might also be put through the mill. The person they had to meet walked into the room. John knew him immediately, having seen him at a public meeting in England before the war. He recognised him as William Joyce, an Englishman and a dedicated Nazi who defected to Germany when war was declared. He was famous (or infamous) for his broadcasts to Britain in which he advocated that British people should join Germany in fighting what the Nazis called the common enemy, communist Russia.

John's turn to be interviewed came and he pretended that he did not speak German and, therefore, needed an interpreter. That gave him more time to think about a question before he answered it. Joyce asked John whether he knew him. John pretended not to know him. Joyce asked him to leave the room while the other POW was interviewed. Joyce's coat was hanging in the waiting room and John grabbed the opportunity to search it. Imagine the tension of those moments with Nazis all around the place who could walk in as he searched that coat. He found a letter addressed to Joyce stating that Dr Goebbels wanted Joyce to interview the POW and put pressure on him to make him co-operate. Joyce was also told to question John to ascertain if he was a genuine sympathiser because, if so, they might be able to use him in Berlin. John's coolness in finding that letter gave him a tremendous advantage because the phrase, "Using him in Berlin", was a reference to an approach that had been made to John to take charge of the Genshagen Holiday Camp - the very thing that the MI6 had instructed him to try to achieve. Despite his efforts to trip him up John played Joyce like a fish.

The other example of the great danger of revealing himself as a spy happened at a meeting to which John had been invited. A group of soldiers from India were there and the Germans were trying to persuade the Indians to join them. An Indian Officer jumped up and made an impassioned speech rejecting all the German offers. When his speech was widely acclaimed, John impulsively rushed forward, shook his hand and immediately realised what a blunder he had made. Joyce was at the meeting and when John turned round, he saw the hatred in his eyes. If Goebbels, the powerful and much feared German Minister for Propaganda, was involved in investigating John, there was no doubt now that John was operating in the top league and a mistake like the one that he had just made could be fatal. John played his cards like that throughout the war and he was only discovered when the Germans found evidence of his activities after Genshagen was closed.

I mentioned that I had been puzzled as to why I had suddenly been moved from Praskovitz to the coalmine. I was only a pawn in the Genshagen set-up and I was surely too small to attract the attention of the Germans unless, of course, the evidence of John Brown's activities contained details of our planned escape. If that evidence, with the names of Benny and me, had come into German hands, they might have thought that we were big fish too – well, a wee bit bigger than prawns anyway. The fact that evidence of some sort was discovered showed that my concerns were justified. When the Gestapo discovered this evidence after Genshagen was closed, they put John on the hit list and word was put out all round Germany that he was a wanted man. The story of how he kept out of their hands is another amazing tale.

I was delighted, however, to read that, when John reached the freedom of a USA Army camp, he referred to his shoes with the documents secreted in them. Later, in the Foreign Office in London, he mentioned that they took his shoes and the papers therein. So John had finally successfully delivered the information that Benny and I had initially been chosen to take back to Britain. This was the information that incriminated Joyce and the members of the British Free Corps. I took a lot of satisfaction from that.

After I was back home, Joyce and the British Free Corps hit the headlines. The famous Treason Trials had started. William Joyce was found guilty and sentenced to be hanged. In his broadcasts from Germany during the war he always opened his broadcast with "Germany calling, Germany calling." He spoke in a very plummy Oxford accent, hence the nickname of Lord Haw Haw, and was much hated by the British public.

John was a key witness in the Treason Trials and his part in bringing Joyce and company to justice made him famous. He was awarded the DCM for his services to MI6. I was delighted for John and it was gratifying for those of us who had put our trust in him with no knowledge of the dangerous work that he was doing.

An amusing thought occurs to me. If Benny and I agreed to work for John, and if John was working for MI6, ergo, did Benny and I also work for MI6? James Bond, stand aside, here I come.

Now that I realise the role that John played and the deeds he did, I feel privileged that he called me his friend. Knowing the risk for him in making a wrong judgement of a person, it humbles me to think how much he was willing to trust me after such a short acquaintance. I only regret that it was just another of my ever recurring 'Almosts', and that fills me with regret and disappointment to this day.

Many people, who misjudged John in Germany, must be saying now, "If I had only known."

I didn't get a chance to say goodbye, John. It was a joy to know you. I would have loved to have had longer to get to know you better.

Appendix B

Hard Luck

By
Alex Clark

A short story based on an experience in a POW camp in Germany in World War 2.

(The story highlighted the value in wartime Czechoslovakia of the contents of the Red Cross parcels in Germany)

It was a bright May morning. The sun, just peeping over the rim of the Schwartz Gebirgen (Black Mountains), was lighting up the river Elbe and the whole valley below. It was a lovely scene. The hills were covered in cherry trees and, as the sun rose in the sky, the blossom on the trees opened up to welcome the morning heat by bursting into a mass of pink puffs as if orchestrated by a conductor. The kind of spring morning that makes you stretch your arms and think how good it is to be alive.

Alan, as he opened his eyes and scratched his flea ridden back, may have welcomed the sun but no way did he feel that it was good to be alive. The first thing that he saw was the pattern made on the ceiling by those damnable symbols of his incarceration, the barbed wire that surrounded the windows. A deep sense of despair enveloped him. A bright morn such as this back home might have seen him setting off for the hills with the enticing prospect of a day's fishing on the mountain lochs. "My God," he thought, "I know now how these coos felt when they stood at the barbed wire fences that prevented them from eating the lush grass in the next field."

These were the dark days in the early part of the Second World War. The German war machine had not yet suffered any major setback and a probable end to the war was very unlikely. For a young conscript so recently torn from the security of "Civvy Street" in Scotland, the prospects looked extremely bleak. In moments such as these, Alan felt that he might forever lose that freedom he had never even remotely appreciated. The Germans were so sure of victory that they were offering favoured positions after the war to those who co-operated. They never defined what they meant by co-operating. Nobody at the camp gave a moment's thought to the offer. Alan now realised how little he had appreciated the joyous days when he could shout to his Mum: "Just off for a walk, Mum, be back soon", bounding away with never a thought to the glorious freedom of it all.

Alan's prison was a working camp beside the beautiful river Elbe in German-occupied Sudetenland. Before the war the building was used as a small Gasthaus (Guesthouse). It was now "home" for about 30 British POW's who had to do hard labour in a stone quarry high in the Schwartz Gebirgen. For "Other Ranks", refusing to work could bring punishment, not least of which was a reduction in rations. For working POW's that was the worst punishment. The normal nosh, described with Teutonic deadpan humour as heavy work rations, was a clear liquid with slight sediment at the bottom. This liquid had a dual function. It served as soup at work and, in the evening, as a reward for a hard day's work, there was a succulent main course of potatoes covered with mouth-watering gravy. The gravy bore a remarkable resemblance to the lunchtime soup.

Any reduction in the heavy work rations could make a man's belly think that his throat had been cut. On a near starvation diet the working conditions in the quarry were pretty grim, especially in winter, when temperatures were well below zero. At least the work took you out into the open air and it broke down the psychological barriers of the "barbed wire madness". Nevertheless it was a poor substitute for freedom, the loss of which Alan felt harder to bear even than the hard labour in the freezing cold of a Central European winter, a winter that brought temperatures so low that bare hands stuck hard to the iron trucks. Pulling your hands away too quickly could tear off skin and flesh. A winter that brought gnawing hunger and throbbing pain from open sores on hands unaccustomed to lifting ice-bound stones.

On a working day Alan hated the early morning period. As the half sleep wore off, the sight of the barbed wire brought an awareness of the awful bleakness of the day, and perhaps of the years, ahead. It was difficult to avoid dwelling too much on what lay ahead, endless such days in incarceration of an unknown duration. It was ironic that his prison was formerly a Guesthouse. It had probably once resounded to the happy laughter of merry holidaymakers. The POW's, feeling not at all merry, set out each morning for the day's work at the quarry. They passed that strict and humourless disciplinarian, the Commandant, who always counted them as though they were sheep going into a pen. Alan had a mental picture of him acting the part of a guesthouse host, calling out "Haste ye back" or a "Hope you enjoy a lovely day ". He could imagine the response. It would have little to do with having a lovely day.

The walk to the quarry was long and difficult. Army boots, long ago worn out, were replaced with wooden clogs. Newspapers wrapped around your feet were a substitute for socks.

Alan's miserable thoughts vanished when he realised that this was to be a very special day, a day that bolstered the spirits and brought a precious reminder that folks at home were thinking of you and your plight. The Red Cross parcels had arrived.

He thought back now to the first arrival of those wonderful Red Cross parcels, that had added such a new dimension to the POW's lives. Although parcels contained no news, they were a contact with home and also a tremendous boost to morale. As many of the men captured on Crete were still suffering malnutrition problems after the horrors of the journey from Crete to Germany, the arrival of the first parcels provided a much-needed addition to the quality and quantity of their food.

The Commandant, always looking for an opportunity to praise the Leader [Adolf Hitler], announced that thanks to the magnanimity of the Leader, permission to distribute the parcels had been given. Being a devout Nazi, he paused for a moment to allow for the expected applause. If he had asked for applause for the Red Cross, the noise would have been deafening. The Commandant did not appreciate the silence that greeted the anticipatory pause. Such gross ingratitude provoked a violent rebuke. He reminded the ungrateful British that the Leader's gesture had been made despite the fact that the British morons had fought against the magnificent army of the Third Reich. An Army, he said, that alone stood between Britain and the threat of the Russian hordes.

Realising that their parcels might be in jeopardy, the lads immediately put on a magnificent show of contrition. To their intense relief, the Hauptman announced that tomorrow (being Sunday and a non-working day) the parcels would be released.

Nobody had ever seen these legendary parcels but rumours of the possible contents reached astronomical proportions. There was a buzz of excitement in the poky little room that night and there was little sleep. "I hope tae guidness they pit in a packet o' fags," says Alan's bosom pal from Shotts in Lanarkshire. "I'm that starvin' I could eat a horse. That fella frae Stalag IVB said that the parcels hae tins o' fags. I'd love to smoke a real fag. Ma throat's that sair smokin' brown paper wrapped up like a fag. A draw on a real fag would be paradise. What an awfie decision, tae smoke them or eat them." Big Geordie shouts out: "I bet you what. If Ian, that sadistic pal o' mine that got away from Crete had a hand in packing the parcels, he'll have stuck a French letter in and be bursting his sides laughing at my language." Poor Geordie! He never got over the shattering discovery that a packet of naval issue condoms, which he had secreted for all that time, had sadly perished. Nobody ever asked him how he discovered the deficiencies.

His optimism was beyond belief on two scores. There was a distinct lack of opportunities to use the content of his packet in the monastic circumstances of POW prison camps and he believed strongly that the war would end soon, allowing him to arrive home with his packet intact. The chatter went on into the wee sma' hours. It reminded Alan of those happy days when he and his brother sat up in bed on Christmas Eve, speculating endlessly on what Santa Claus might bring. It was hard to believe that these men, scarcely able to contain their excitement about the contents of a parcel, were the hardened veterans of the Greece and Crete battles, men who had seen and experienced unspeakable horrors in action. Oh my! How starvation, deprivation, loss of liberty, dignity and self-respect can create such havoc with the emotions of even the toughest of men.

Morning arrived at last. What a scene! No child ever awaited the arrival of Santa Claus with more expectation than those men did when Santa, disguised as a German Commandant, arrived to oversee the distribution of the famous parcels. Truth to tell, he was bursting with curiosity to see the contents. No Christmas stocking ever matched the outpouring from the cornucopia in the guise of these humdrum brown boxes.

With mounting excitement those prosaic tins were pulled out. A short time ago in Civvy Street nobody would have given the tins a second glance in the counter of a local shop. Now they were a symbol of plenty. The Commandant watched goggle-eyed at goods that had long ago disappeared from German shops. The Angels at home who packed the parcels would have shed tears of gratification if they had heard the boyish shouts of delight. Each tin was held up for all to see, despite the fact that they all held identical contents. Cheers rang out for corned beef, that hitherto unpopular army dish, cheers for coffee, tea, fruit pudding, dried egg, sausages etc., etc. No pirates' horde could have produced more emotion than these common-or-garden items which circumstances elevated to the status of luxuries. Alan's thoughts went back to one of the many pearls of wisdom from his old granny, "hunger, my laddie, is the best sauce."

Hunger can relate to more than food. The loudest roar of acclamation was given to a tin that contained that unhealthy, choking, filthy but delightful weed – fags, fags, glorious fags, all 50 of them in the famous Gold Flake tin. What a grip the mighty weed had. In those days there was no question of it being anti-social. It never entered a smoker's mind to give up the habit. Indeed a non-smoker was very much the odd man out in company. The grip it had really did surface in a POW camp, where fags were unattainable. Before the parcels arrived, it was not uncommon for a desperate few to roll up cigarettes from sawdust and brown paper and nearly choke to death after a few puffs. In no time at all, Alan and his cronies really enjoyed their goodies, oblivious to the thick smog they were creating.

Alan shook off the nostalgic thoughts of those early days. Red Cross parcels were coming quite regularly now. Their original objective of supplementing the rations that were desperately deficient in the early days was still very important. But by 1942 they had become much more than a supplement to the standard prison rations. The rations for the German population were also very meagre. The plight of the occupied and slave populations was even worse. As the Germans stormed through on the Eastern Front they uprooted thousands of Czechs, Poles and Slavs. They brought back many of them to use as slave labour, releasing German soldiers for service on the Eastern Front. Food for all these dispossessed people was very scarce. The Czechs and their families still in Sudetenland were perhaps even worse off. Luxuries such as real (not ersatz) coffee and tea, chocolate, etc., were almost unknown. Although bartering the contents of the parcels was strictly forbidden, POW's sometimes used luxury items to acquire civvy clothes for planned escapes or to exchange them for fresh food, such as fruit.

This was an exciting day for Alan. He was expecting to get a very special item. The contents of Red Cross parcels were very precious to POW's, so barter was not a common activity. It was a different matter in civilian Germany. There the scarcity of food meant that black market activities were rife.

Black marketing was a very serious offence and carried a heavy penalty. Civilians, particularly those from occupied zones, had to be extremely careful. Alan had befriended a Czech civilian who worked with him at the quarry face. Anton was a huge and powerful man. Often he would come to Alan's assistance when he saw him unsuccessfully trying to break up a particularly large stone. With one deft flick of his big sledgehammer, Anton would smash it into smithereens. They became great friends.

Anton had a wee lass of only two years old. When Alan learned she had never tasted real chocolate and that her third birthday was coming soon, he parted with some of his precious chocolate. The big man was overcome. Life under the German jackboot had few happy moments and this would be a highlight of the wee one's birthday. In return Anton wanted to smuggle in something special for Alan but, because the risk to Anton and his family would be too great, Alan refused. When pressed, he said there was one small thing that could pass the search and for which he had a real yen. Prison food was seldom fresh, especially the parcel food, appreciated though it was. It was obvious, for example, that an egg in a tin had to be the powdered version.

Alan, like most of the prisoners had fantasies about food, a bit like those of a pregnant woman, irrational but very compelling. His favourite torture was to dream of eating a Scottish high tea, consisting of a huge plate of lovely crispy bacon, sausages and fried bread. In the centre of this feast was Alan's "piece de resistance", a beautiful golden soft fried egg. The greatest paintings in the world paled into insignificance beside that masterpiece in Alan's fantasy. He told Anton that a nice fresh egg would be a real treat.

Anton lived near a farm and, although eggs had a high value on the black market, he managed to sneak a couple into the quarry. Today was the big day. Alan tried not to appear too excited. He was actually quite anxious that something might go wrong. He now wished that he had not asked for it. The chance of Anton being caught was slight but even a small thing such as an egg could mean big trouble if the police caught him.

Today it is difficult to imagine that the prospect of a fresh egg could generate such excitement, but the titillating prospect of cooking that egg really excited Alan. The others showed an interest too, more because of the challenge of fooling the guards. Searches could be very intensive. Alan kept up the excitement, rabbiting on for ages about the big occasion when he would break a fresh egg on the top of the wood-burning stove. Of course, there were no cooking facilities in the camp. He couldn't wait to watch it spreading slowly until it formed a perfect circle. But if the guards found the egg, Alan might have plenty time to fantasise in solitary confinement.

Anton handed over the eggs at the end of the day. The path down the mountain was very steep and rough. Wooden clogs made it even more precarious. Alan, with the eggs under his forage cap, proceeded gingerly down the bumpy path. His acrobatic efforts to keep his head on an even keel to prevent the eggs bouncing about inside his cap brought hoots of laughter from his pals. The guard was puzzled at the hilarity but he had long ago given up trying to understand the most peculiar British humour. An hour later they arrived back at the camp. Alan, stiff and sore of neck with his balancing act, was slightly less enthusiastic about his culinary dream. He was still determined to clear the last hurdle, the body search. The lads had agreed that they would not take anything into camp that day because even modest catches by the guard could result in an intensified search. Fortunately the guard was less vigilant than usual and passed them through unscathed. A big cheer went up as they entered the quarters. Cheers greeted every successful evasion with glee, even a lowly egg.

Alan's big moment arrived. They had smuggled in extra wood to supplement the meagre fuel ration. The wood burner was stoked up. Alan smeared some grease on his Dixie then produced one of the famous eggs. The shout went up "Come on lads, Jock's about to fry his fresh egg." Quite an audience sat up in bed to watch the culmination of all Alan's efforts. With a proper sense of the drama of the occasion, Alan raised the egg aloft then gently tapped it on the side of the Dixie. The egg stayed intact. Another tap, but slightly firmer this time – still no result. Somebody shouted: "Damn thick shells on Sudetenland eggs, must feed those hens on a mixture of bran and cement." Alan, highly embarrassed, gave it a rare old whack and the shell shattered. A huge roar of laughter burst out. Poor Alan, he could not believe his eyes. After all he had done to get a fresh egg, all the head balancing, the tension of the daily body search, the vision of the egg slowly spreading as it cooked; after everything, all was in vain. The egg was hard-boiled! Hard luck, Alan.

Appendix C

The Royal Marines

I found out from a book I read a long, long time after the war that Major Garret of the Royal Marines was left behind at Sphakia. He managed to find a landing craft that had been beached after the evacuation. Accompanied by 4 Officers and 134 other ranks, he successfully reached the North African coast near Tobruck. Our Radio Direction Finder Unit came under Major Garret's command. I was separated from my RDF Unit and sent back up the line to join the Marines taking part in the last rearguard action, otherwise I could probably have escaped with Major Garret - another of my "Almost Syndromes"? I was a bit envious when I first heard of their successful escape and thought how unlucky I was to have missed the chance to go with them. I heard afterwards that some of my comrades, whom I thought so lucky to be evacuated or to have escaped with Major Garret, were posted to Tobruck in the North African desert. Very sadly some were killed at Tobruck. I thought that I was unlucky. One's fortunes in war are a lottery.

Appendix D

Post-War Visit to Sponsors of a Red Cross Parcel

It would never have occurred to the people who sponsored a Red Cross Parcel that some of them contained not only much appreciated food but also could be used as currency. A card was often enclosed in a parcel containing the name and address of the sponsor. After the War, it was my good fortune to be able to contact a group called the Girls Guildry who had sponsored one of my parcels. I asked whether I could meet them to tell them personally how much their parcel meant to me in the difficult days in a POW camp in Germany in 1941.

I thought that the story of my first meeting with them might amuse you. I knew about the Girl Guides so I assumed that the Guildry was an English version of the Guides. They lived near Dunstable in Bedfordshire and agreed to meet me at Luton railway station. I expected that one or more of their parents would escort them. When I got down from the train, there was no sign of a group of wee lassies with their parents. Although I was now demobbed, I agreed to wear my Marine Blues so that I would be easily recognised. Just as I began to wonder whether I had messed up the arrangement, a group of nice looking young ladies came up the platform, wreathed in smiles. They seemed to be heading for me but they were not wee lassies so I was fair bamboozled, not for long. The Guildry were actually former Girl Guides. All these years in a monastic state and here I was strolling down the street with half a dozen nice young ladies. A friendship developed and it exists to this day.

Some time after my visit, a group of them were passing through Glasgow on holiday and called at my parents' home to see me. My Mum was taken aback and wondered whether I had been over enthusiastic after my years of monastic existence. I took them, yes all of them, to a local cinema to see the latest film. Mairi, the Usherette, knew me well. She probably thought that she did not know me all that well when she saw my entourage. She nearly swallowed her tonsils in her utter amazement but she quickly recovered her composure. Twigging that it was most unlikely that I had acquired half a dozen new girl friends and was in a dither about which one to take to the pictures, She said: "Your usual back seat, Alex?" Mairi always had a wicked sense of humour so she made sure that the story was well publicised and the story of Alex and his secret harem from England took a long time to die down. My girl friend took even longer to speak to me again.

What a lovely ending to a story that started in a POW camp in Czechoslovakia, ending up in Bedfordshire almost four years later. Indeed, it has not ended because I am still in contact with two of these now not so young but still nice looking ladies, Olive Blackburn and Rene Deeks.

Appendix E

The Seaborne Invasion That Never Was

I wrote that I was puzzled why our Royal Marine Unit (MNBDO) were kept on guard at the beach Canea. We assumed that a seaborne invasion was expected but it never materialised. At Maleme Airport and elsewhere help was desperately needed. I had first hand information from Australian and New Zealand lads who fought on these Fronts and whom I met later in POW camps that they asked the same question. As you know, I followed a policy of introducing as few historical references to my story as possible because I wanted to tell the story with only the knowledge that I had at the time. However, I recently read an analysis of the situation at Canea in a book by Antony Beevor, "Crete – The Battle and the Resistance". It was so relevant to my situation at Canea that, now that I have finished my story, I decided that the reader would be interested in one historical explanation of why we were held at Canea.

Antony Beevor comments that a decision by General Freyberg to hold the Welch Regiment at Canea had a dramatic affect on the course of the Battle. Beevor's research revealed a high level (Ultra) signal from London to General Freyberg. The signal was:-

"The Seaborne Invasion. Signal to General Freyberg on 21st May. Ultra signal OL 15/389. Personal to General Freyberg – most immediate. On continuation of the attack Colorada [Crete], reliably reported that among operations planned for May [by the Germans] is air landing two mountain battalions and attack Canea. Landing from echelon of small ships depending on situation at sea."

Beevor draws attention to the full stop between the two sentences. It separates the words, "attack Canea" and "Landing". Freyberg apparently had a firm conviction that the invasion would come from the sea. Beevor feels that this conviction might have made him confused so that he missed the full stop and concluded that "attack Canea" meant an attack from the sea instead of from the Air. Beevor quoted the following order that Freyberg issued after receiving the Ultra signal:-

"Reliable information. Early Seaborne attack in area Canea likely. New Zealand Division remains responsible coast from West to Kladiso River. Welch Battalion to stiffen existing defences from Kladiso to Halepa."

Beevor suggests that this signal supports his theory.

I have written of how puzzled I was that we were held at the beach at Canea during all the fighting at Maleme Airport. We waited in vain on Canea beach for that seaborne attack and the defenders of Maleme Airport waited in vain for assistance. Looking back to those terrible days which had such disastrous and momentous affects on the lives of so many people, it is so hard to accept that the fate of the Battle of Crete might have hung on a dot on a piece of paper. Many factors have influenced the course of battles throughout history but surely omitting to note a period between two sentences must be unique. If Beevor's conclusions are accurate, General Freyberg, known as a soldier's General, must have suffered hell if he learnt that his interpretation of the Ultra signal was incorrect because he forgot a full stop at the end of a sentence

Appendix F

(An Extract from an Official Historical Account of the Last Rearguard Action and the Surrender at Sphakia)

This extract contains more information that I learned after the War. It had a direct influence on events in which I was involved. It gives a detailed analysis of the last rearguard action and the surrender of Crete. I was tempted to use it in my story of those events at Sphakia in Chapter 5 and 6, but I stuck to my objective of not using knowledge gained after the war. I thought, however, that readers might be interested in the historical accounts of these events so I have included in this Appendix a detailed analysis of what happened there and why it happened. It was described in the book, titled "Greece and Crete 1941", written by Christopher Buckley and published in 1952 at the request of HM Government.

For example, I did not know at the time the exact location of the front line. Long after the war I read in this book that the final rearguard took place at a village called Vitsilokoumos. (I describe in Appendix G a visit to Crete in 1987. I could find no trace of a village of Vitsikoloumos. I have read that some villages on Crete were razed to the ground as punishment for resistance activity. Perhaps Vitsikoloumos was such a village.) I was fascinated by the description in the book of the situation when the last rearguard action and the surrender took place. It confirms my version of some of the events as I described them. It gives a detailed historical and military analysis that I could not possibly have known. I feel that my decision to describe my feelings and emotions from a lowly viewpoint without knowledge gained after the war has brought about a juxtaposition of the two versions, the emotional and the historical, and makes an interesting comparison.

Buckley wrote:-

"General Weston, in conference with his three brigadiers, at one o'clock that afternoon [May 29th], decided that the Saucer [Askifou] could be held until nightfall by the 4th New Zealand Brigade which would then retire to the coast. The Australians with the Royal Marine Battalion would take up a final defensive position at Vitsilokoumos, a particularly strong defensive position where the road winds and narrows rather more than two miles northeast of Sphakia. They would have the three remaining tanks and three Bren carriers under command. Layforce and the 5th New Zealand Brigade would move south to the dispersal area and the beach.

Still the Germans refrained from pressing the pursuit. The forward New Zealand position covering the Northern approach to Askifou was engaged by the enemy advance guard in the afternoon but managed to hold the attack without difficulty. For the second day in succession there was comparatively little air activity except when sixty German aircraft delivered a heavy attack upon Sphakia and the adjacent beaches between 6 and 7 p.m.

As the evening haze began to gather, a powerful convoy of ships approached the coast of Crete. It arrived off Sphakia about 10 p.m. Here was the troopship Glengyle, the cruisers Phoebe and Perth, the A.A. cruisers Calcutta and Coventry, and the destroyers Jarvis, Janis and Hasty. Pickets had been posted at the various approaches at the beaches to prevent a repetition of the gate-crashing incidents of the previous night, and if the system of embarkation proved somewhat inelastic and produced occasional vexatious delays before the units taken off could be assembled, it at least avoided the dangers of uncontrolled embarkation. Naval Officers were sent on shore to explain the procedure, and the vital necessity for absolute stillness in the event of enemy planes coming over to drop flares. The quiet and business-like way in which the naval men spoke seemed to brace everyone's nerves and to give them renewed confidence.

For more than three hours on that still night the large flat-bottomed, shallow-draught boats plied backwards and forwards across glass-smooth waters under the tranquil summer sky. In almost total silence the weary, stumbling khaki-clad figures limped aboard the ships, some still carrying their rifles, some without them. When the time for putting to sea arrived shortly after 3.a.m., 6,500 men who fought at Maleme and Canea had been taken aboard. Whatever might happen subsequently it had already been possible for the Royal Navy to lift a larger number of men from the island than had been contemplated by Freyberg three days earlier.

German aircraft were soon overhead next morning and hunted the convoy for several hours but, except that H.M.A.S. Perth received a hit in a boiler room and suffered some casualties, the attackers met with no success. In the later stages of the passage a few long-fighters flew to see the convoy home.

On the morning of 30th May over 10,000 men still remained concentrated around Sphakia and on the ten mile stretch of the road to the north. It had been planned that four destroyers should be despatched that night to complete the evacuation but as these could only convey 2,000 men between them, Admiral Cunningham now agreed to extend the evacuation by another night, seeing that some R.A.F. fighter cover was available for part of the return passage.

Vasey, who was in command of the rearguard on the road to Sphakia, determined to hold the attackers off his main position at Vitsikoloumos by making full use of his tanks and carriers in a delaying action. It would be their task to cover the successive demolitions in turn, deal with motor cyclists who normally formed the reconnaissance element of the German advance, and subsequently to fall back when the enemy pushed forward in some strength. There did indeed appear to be a good opportunity for the armoured fighting vehicles to engage an enemy vanguard that was unlikely at first to enjoy much assistance from support weapons, and in its way the day's fighting proved to be a rather neat and satisfactory business.

Before 7 am. the two leading companies of No 10 Mountain

Regiment, having pushed on past the Askifou Plain, began their attack. Contrary to expectations they were supported by three light tanks, and one of the British tanks was speedily knocked out. The other two withdrew behind the first of the demolitions which had been prepared by the 42nd Field Company RE.

The new position which they took up after the demolition had been blown was about a mile south of Imvros at a point where a bend on the road concealed our tanks from view while providing good observation of the southern edge of the village ……

By 5pm. the two tanks were back in the main Australian [and the Royal Marines] position. But both were finished. They had steering, brake, engine and clutch troubles and so they were ditched in positions where their ruined hulls would help to strengthen the existing roadblocks. The Germans made contact before dark, but the commander of No. 100 Mountain Regiment was sufficiently impressed with the natural strength of the position to refrain from attacking it. He gave orders for a company to move out on either flank during the night so as to effect an envelopment at dawn next morning.

During the day two Sunderland flying boats had arrived at Sphakia and, in accordance with orders from Middle East Command, General Freyberg and his staff were taken off, General Weston being left in charge of the final stage of evacuation.

It was perhaps the deepest tragedy in Freyberg's life. Through no fault of his own the battle had been lost which above all others he would have wished to have won. He had been in supreme command and his New Zealanders had endured the longest and the severest part of the fighting and without any means of countering the deadly and persistent air assaults of the enemy they had been powerless to turn the fortunes of the day.

The problem of rations and water had become acute. The Australians posted on the crest of the ridge, a good two-hour climb from Sphakia, were already suffering acutely from the shortage, and the supply of rations on the beach at Sphakia was not large …..

When Saturday 31st May dawned, there was still something like 9,000 troops left on the island, concentrated on a very small area covering Sphakia. Of this number, less than half were fighting troops. This category comprised approximately 1,100 New Zealanders, 1,250 Australians, 550 Marines, and 500 Layforce. The Australian rearguard at Vitsilokoumos held positions on either side of the road in considerable strength. On their right Layforce (until relieved by the Royal Marines and the Maori battalion) formed a defensive flank. On their left elements of the New Zealand brigades were in position. The commander of the No. 100 Mountain Regiment according to his own account, finding that our front was more extended than he supposed and that neither of his two flanking companies actually overlapped the defence, decided on a wider enveloping movement …...

Nothing seemed more surprising at the time than the failure of the enemy to take advantage of the situation by dropping parachutists at Sphakia and thereby deranging and perhaps preventing our evacuation. The Germans knew perfectly well, from the evidence of their aircraft, that the whole of our force from Maleme-Canea-Suda was making for that tiny fishing village. A comparatively small number of airborne troops could have seized and held the place and stood a good chance of destroying our troops piecemeal as they came from struggling across the Cretan mountains. Yet this was not done. Perhaps the explanation lay in the fact that they had no more parachutists immediately available for such an operation. If so, this was the result of the heavy losses we had inflicted on them during the struggle.

That as it happened, was not the worst of Weston's anxieties during the day. Wireless communication with Middle East command was now only intermittent, and Creforce was under the impression that evacuation was not to be extended to cover the night of June 1st/2nd. But during the afternoon a signal came through to say that the last evacuation would take place on the coming night. It was hoped to send enough shipping to embark 3,600, and a couple of Sunderlands would also be sent, in one of which Weston himself was instructed to leave.

[Author's note: -This confirms the story that I told about the order to prepare a marker beacon for the Sunderlands coming in at night. The marker was sited on the flank on the hill at the front at Vitsilokoumos. The danger that we were in of being mortar bombed by the Germans if even a match was lit prompted one Australian to shout that he would shoot the first bastard who tried to light the beacon.]

It needed no very elaborate calculations to discern that something like 5,500 men would still be left behind when the ships drew away from Sphakia for the last time. The problem of feeding those troops still retained was already causing the utmost anxiety, for the remaining rations were not sufficient to provide for the force beyond that day. Already the men were on short commons and many were desperately hungry. Continued resistance at this stage depended more upon food than upon ammunition. Weston signalled Middle East Command to this effect in the early evening and asked for a directive. But the batteries of the remaining wireless set in the cave at Sphakia were now failing and no reply was ever received,

The decision to abandon some 20 per cent of the defenders of Crete had not been lightly taken. While humanity prompted that every possible effort should be made to rescue these long suffering troops, the dangers of sending more shipping yet again into those waters had to be taken into account. It would be no act of humanity and a poor economy of force if more men were to be lost in attempting the rescue than could be saved by extending the evacuation over a further night. But transcending this was a wider consideration of Mediterranean strategy. It was not only the lives of the men in Malta, the men in Tobruck, conceivably also the men in Cyprus. Let the Royal Navy once be weakened beyond a certain point and the consequences were beyond all computation. It was said of Jellicoe in the previous world war that he was the only man who could have lost the war in a single afternoon. Admiral Cunningham in the present conflict shouldered a responsibility scarcely less awful.

The decision had to be taken. Everything available was to be scraped together for that night's evacuation. After that the ships would not return.

At eleven o'clock that night they arrived—the cruiser Phoebe, the minelayer Abdiel, the destroyer Jackal, Kimberley and Hotspur, Three landing-craft had been left behind after the previous night's evacuation. Dragged ashore they remained concealed in caves all day. Now they were loaded up with the first troops to leave.

The order of embarkation allowed for the passage of the remainder of the 4th New Zealand Brigade, the 5th New Zealand Brigade, the 29th Australian Brigade, Layforce and the Royal Marine Battalion in that priority. Strong guards had been posted at the beach approaches in order to ensure this priority for the organised formations and to prevent the boats being swamped by any undisciplined rush of stragglers and others. It had to be done.

At first all went smoothly, the New Zealanders were embarked in an orderly manner, and the timetable seemed to be well ahead of schedule. But the news got round that this was the last night of evacuation, and more and more men, seeing the certainty of capture if they were left behind, surged towards the beaches – confusion reigned. It was rendered worse by the fact that the Navy on each of the previous nights had been able to lift numbers in excess of its estimate. This led to extra troops being allowed to station themselves at the approach to the beach so as to be within summons. As a result the men of Layforce found themselves unable to break their way through the rabble of refugees. The Australians [the Royal Marines, the Maoris and other troops] who had held the final position on the escarpment found themselves impeded in the same way. When the ships sailed at 3 a.m. they carried 4,050 men, a figure that exceeded the estimate by 400.

Before leaving by air, in accordance with his instructions from Middle East Command, General Weston had issued the following instructions to Lieut.-Colonel Colvin of Layforce, the senior officer remaining on the island:

In view of the following facts:

(a) My orders direct me to give preference to fighting troops. This has reduced the active garrison below what is required for resistance.

(b) No rations are left this Saturday night. Most of the troops are too weak owing to shortage of food and heavy strain to organise further resistance.

(c) The wireless will give out in a few hours and the risk of waiting for instructions from Middle East cannot be accepted, as this will leave the officer in charge without any guidance as to his course of action.

(d) There is no possibility of further evacuation.

I, therefore, direct you to collect such senior officers as are available in the early hours of tomorrow morning and transmit these orders to the senior of them.

These orders direct this officer to contact the enemy and to capitulate.

The sum of £1,000 was handed over to Colvin so that individual groups of men might be able to purchase means of escape.

The decision to surrender came as a thunderclap to the majority of the troops when Colonel Colvin and his officers informed them that no alternative remained. Attempts were made to tear down the white flag that was hoisted above Sphakia as an indication to German troops and aircraft that the end had come. The hope that springs eternal, and never more certainly than among men in the extremist danger, had led some to believe that there would yet be one further night of evacuation - nor was this unreasonable in view of the repeated changes which the time-table had undergone. But when it was realised that the rations were exhausted, and that small arms ammunition also was running out, the situation had to be accepted. No serious defence would have been possible against the assault which a conscientious but unimaginative German commander, fighting, like Tybalt, 'by the book of arithmetic', was planning against men too weary and weak with hunger to crawl forward and surrender. Foreseeing this, and foreseeing also that the German advanced forces would have carried no superfluous stocks of food with them, Weston immediately upon his arrival at Alexandria had signalled Middle East Command requesting that sufficient food be dropped by air at least to enable the men to march as far as some locality where the Germans might be expected to feed them. This was done without delay.

Before the final evacuation General Wavell had sent the following signal to Major-General Weston, RM, the commander of the rearguard.

You know the heroic effort the Navy has made to rescue you. I hope that you will be able to get away most of those that remain, but this is the last night the Navy can come. Please tell those that have to be left that the fight put up against such odds has won the admiration of us all and every effort to bring them back is being made. General Freyberg has told me how magnificently your Marines have fought and of your own grand work. I have heard also of the heroic fighting of young Greek soldiers. I send you my grateful thanks."

Appendix G

In Search of Lost Memories

I paid a visit to Crete in 1998 in the company of Alex Sinclair. So many things did not surface in the writing of this book that I thought, before it was published, a visit to the places involved might bring back memories. The following is an article I wrote about the trip:-

I had finished writing a book about my war experiences in the Second World War from 1939 to 1945. Keeping diaries in the Forces in wartime was forbidden so the story was dependent on my memory, a function that never was very efficient even before the ageing process knocked it for six. Psychiatrists tell us nowadays that difficult and traumatic conditions can drive memories deep down. If loss of memory can be attributed to traumatic conditions, goodness knows where memories are driven if, in addition to trauma, you add the normal lapse of memory caused by the ageing process over a period of 57 years. The combination of these two factors makes me wonder that I had any story left to tell.

As I was involved in the withdrawal across the mountains I had much to write about. I was concerned at the number of times that I had to state: "I cannot recall what happened———". I decided to return to Crete and walk over the White Mountain tracks again. I hoped that the warmth of sunny days would perhaps bring memories to the surface - what a crummy excuse for a Mediterranean holiday in the spring!

My friend, Alex Sinclair, overheard me discussing some of my planning difficulties, in particular the problem of a car. At age 77 I was well past my sell-by date and I had no experience of driving on the right hand side of the road. Absentmindedly driving up the wrong side is a habit frowned upon on most roads but on the mountainous roads of Crete, with precipitous drops into deep gorges, it could be a lethal weakness.

The youthful Alex, at least youthful compared to me, had previous experience of Cretan roads and, with a rush of blood and probably after a few drams, he offered not only to accompany me to Crete but also to drive the car. It crossed my mind to ask him what sort of experiences of Crete he had encountered but in face of his generous offer I forbore.

I was a bit rusty (and perhaps rustic) on the preparation for a stay in the heat of the Eastern Mediterranean. I had decided to have a wee dummy run in selecting the appropriate clobber both for the hot weather and for whatever Arctic conditions might be prevalent in Scotland on departure and on arrival home. When the two beds in the spare bedroom could hold no more, I knew that a fair degree of culling was required.

I was lucky that Alex was still very experienced in matters relating to foreign travel and I only entered the arena when he had done all the donkeywork and handed me the tickets. There are some advantages to being considered somewhat senile.

One piece of advice that Alex gave me was to order some Greek coinage for use when we landed in Crete and also not to leave it too late in ordering travellers cheques. I ordered £75 worth of drachmas and £250 of the cheques. I got a nice feeling when I worked out how many drachmas amounted to at an exchange rate of roughly 520 drachmas to the pound. It was the nearest I have been to a millionaire. I wondered how many thousand drachmas would be a reasonable tip.

All this planning started way back in October but in no time the big day arrived. As we approached Aberdeen Airport I was warned to have the flight tickets, boarding pass when we checked in and, on pain of instant return home, my passport. Despite desperate culling, my bag weighed a ton. I also had a grip for an overnight stay in London and a light raincoat in case of snow in London, an absolute pessimist!

The first stage of the journey was no bother. We joined the queue for checking in. I was aware of the shortage of pockets in my summer clothing in which to place documents and money that would be needed at short notice, such as passport. I checked that sterling, drachmas, tickets, passport and wallet were all put in a readily accessible order, or so I thought.

During my preparations for packing I came across a relic from the past, a wee trolley for pulling your suitcase. It was a sort of zimmer on two wheels and when folded up it strapped neatly onto the suitcase. After I plonked my suitcase on the scales at the reception desk, I picked up my grip and coat ready to move off when I was told that my wee trolley was considered to be passenger luggage. I fumbled about like mad to remove the trolley that now had to be carried. All my organised planning now descended into chaos.

I noticed Alex doing his best to look as if he didn't know me from Adam. A boarding pass was now added to the multifarious documents that had to be ready at the toot and so far I hadn't even seen an aeroplane to board!

Alex's planning would have done credit to the D-Day landing. We had seats near the exit and on either side of the aisles. It was easier to get out of your seat when going to the toilet or when disembarking without squeezing out of the close packed seats and constant apologising for tramping on toes. I fastened my seat belt and relaxed. Then came that miracle of logistics, a full meal served from a trolley with only inches to spare on either side. The meal must be served, consumed and the residue cleared away before the plane approaches the destination. On a relatively short journey from Aberdeen to London that is no mean feat.

Those of you who have not travelled on an economy ticket would be amazed at the speed and organisation at which the meal is served. It consists of a starter, a main course, a dessert, biscuits, cheese, butter, sugar, milk and all the cups, glasses and cutlery, all pre-packed and presented on the space of one little tray.

An equally logistical miracle is required of the uninitiated traveller to cope with unravelling all of this, in the correct order, and to find a space on the tray to do it. It crossed my mind to ask for a simple wee sandwich. I was doing quite well until the stewardess came along with the tea. It was in an ordinary teapot!

I held out my cup to be filled just at the moment when the stewardess was distracted by someone wanting to squeeze past the minuscule space at the side of the trolley. I congratulate British Airways on the temperature of the tea because I love my tea nice and hot. I was less impressed, however, when the stewardess missed my cup and the scalding hot tea landed on a very sensitive part of my anatomy. I managed to repress a loud scream.

I had chosen a nice golden shade of trouser in anticipation of warm weather. I had not quite envisaged this. The contrite solicitation from stewardesses only partially made up for the pain. Stained wet breeks in that particular place was embarrassing and I was worried that I would not be able cross my hands over to hide it because I was carrying so much luggage. Fortunately I was given a special wee clootie that cleared up the stain.

A poor start to my foreign trip and I was barely out of Aberdeen! As we left the plane, I was given lovely smiles from the stewardesses. I could swear that they were striving not to gaze at the part of my anatomy that had been given the hot cuppa.

We had to stay overnight in London so Alex chose a hotel described as being in the Gatwick airport complex. You could have squeezed Ballater into a corner of the place and we walked for miles along corridors that seemed to have no ending before we reached the hotel. If I had been on my own, I would have needed a bobbin of thread to find my way back to the airport. Next morning we completed the formalities of checking in and sat down to await the call to board the plane.

The place was seething with people. Many were passing time sitting around, others were milling around the shops and many were rushing around at a high rate of knots. A number were the well-dressed business types, carrying briefcases and the minimum of up-market luggage. Probably many were members of organisations with access to staff and special lounges to attend to all the problems that plague lesser mortals in the economy class on charter flights. The former were well organised and seemed to know exactly where they were going. Fortunately so did Alex so I followed him like a wee dog on a leash.

It was interesting to observe all the different attitudes of travellers, some glancing anxiously at the large Departure Board no doubt worried stiff that they would miss their plane, others obviously experienced travellers, were sleeping or reading. Stressed mothers, like hens with runaway chicks, were calling to young children to stay close. A microcosm of life's emotions. I pondered on the possible purpose of their journeys, on the feelings they might experience on arrival at their destinations. Would it be the pleasure of a restful holiday, the joy of a reunion, the sadness of a parting, the grief of a funeral, perhaps even the seeking of peace of mind in a new life in a long sought Arcadia?

Finally, we boarded our plane. I was interested to note that the airline was British Caledonia. When I travelled regularly between Edinburgh and London in the Sixties, British Airways had the monopoly of that route until British Caledonia entered the fray with cheaper and better services. I was pleased to see that the stewardesses still wore smart tartan outfits and gave the same cheerful and helpful service. Nonetheless, I decided to keep a close eye on the teapot.

The plane journey would take just over three hours. I thought back to my first journey to Crete in 1941. It took many weeks. The convoy had sailed from Glasgow via Nova Scotia and South Africa to Egypt, where we joined another ship to sail to Crete. By contrast, now we had a G&T and another pre-packed meal with a bottle of wine and we were almost over Crete. As we approached the island I could see the high mountains and I could feel excitement mounting at the prospect of the challenge of the week ahead.

We stepped off the plane into a lovely sunny day. Despite the awkwardness of carrying it with all my luggage, I had brought my old straw hat all the way from Aberdeen and now, as I relished the warm sunshine, I perched it in its proper place at a jaunty angle on my head. A hired car awaited us and soon we were on our way to our hotel in Plakias on the South coast of the Island. It was late evening when we arrived and the light was already beginning to fade because European time is two hours ahead of British time. There was still enough light to see that Plakias was beautifully situated in a bay with views across the Libyan Sea and a backcloth of magnificent mountains.

In 1941 Plakias had been a small fishing village. Tourism was now its main occupation and hotels and restaurants lined the promenade that ran around the bay. Identification of places I had been to during the war was going to be difficult. That was a matter for another day.

The hotel was situated just above the village, in the foothills of the mountains that soared into the night sky. We stood for a moment to gaze out over the bay and the Libyan Sea, the sun setting behind the hills. It was breathtakingly beautiful. No wonder Zeus and his gods and goddesses chose Crete as their earthly home.

We were tired after our journey but the promenade was ablaze with lights, their reflection on the water and the coloured lights outside the restaurants drew us like a magnet. In minutes Alex and I were sitting at the sea front sampling our first bottle of Greek wine.

My mind drifted back to 1941 and that very different scene at Sphakia, a few miles up the road from Plakias. How little we ever know of what the future holds for us.

Our holiday had been booked with a firm called 'Simply Crete', who evidently had elderly geezers like me in mind when they devised the 'Simply' bit. They had arranged for us to have a hired car for the week. We decided Alex should spend some time getting to terms with the right hand drive. The comments in the brochure about driving conditions on Crete had persuaded him that it might be wise to use the first day to check whether the mountain roads were as bad as reputed. At a briefing next morning the representative of 'Simply

Crete' answered Alex's question about the state of the road to Sphakia. I hoped to revive some memories at Sphakia of the evacuation of thousands of British troops when the Battle of Crete was deemed lost. She answered that the road was not too bad but that we should be careful on some of the higher roads where there had been landslides and parts of the roads had slipped down the hill. "Just be careful", she said in a very matter of fact voice. If Alex was ever so slightly apprehensive perhaps you would appreciate his feelings if I give you a little extract from 'Simply Crete's' brochure, with its confidence booster on driving on the island:-

The key to driving in Crete is to remember that even if you obey the rules, other people not only may not know them, but if they did, they would not respect them. Caution is therefore essential at all times. Here are a few tips that we think may help.

When driving along the national highways it is the custom if you are driving slowly to pull out over into the slow lane across the white line. Staying in the middle will only irritate the drivers behind you who are expecting you to pull over and let them past. Be very wary though, if driving in the slow lane round a blind bend, as you may find something parked and blocking your way.'

We picked up the hired car. It was a well-used little Suzuki with manual gears and an acceleration capability that required you to give plenty of notice to the occasional Cretan on a donkey that intended to overtake you. If Alex was just a wee bit edgy, it was excusable when you recall he was used to an automatic Mercedes. The terrain was not calculated to calm the nerves. An elderly geezer like me as navigator did not help, especially when the traffic signs were in Greek, so we were often on the wrong road because it took me so long to interpret them.

The mountains towered over Plakias and immediately we started to climb up over the steep hairpin bends. High up on the mountain, the small village of Sellia, with it's sparkling white houses glistening in the strong sunlight, seemed to be balanced precariously on the edge of the road. The cliffs around the Bay protected Plakias like a mother protecting her child. Beyond them the shimmering sea stretched south to the horizon, its smoothness broken only by the hilly island of Nisos Gavtos away in the distance.

The warnings of the 'Simply Crete' brochure, and of their representative, to beware of the cavalier attitude of Cretan drivers was soon substantiated and our decision to take a day to become familiar with Cretan roads was evidently justified. Any idea of sightseeing as we drove up the mountain roads was shattered, since great concentration was called for.

You never knew what danger lurked just around any one of the innumerable blind hairpin bends. The narrow roads could suddenly become even narrower as a result of landslides that left gaps as if a monster had taken huge bites out of them. Large stones were pushed carelessly to the side of the road and everyone except us drove on the wrong side.

Warning signs were very scarce. No doubt Cretan drivers, perhaps fed from youth on a diet of mythological stories of heroic deeds of Homeric proportions, considered that all these hazards were scarcely worth a mention. They seemed to revel in the challenges. All Cretans had high standards of hospitality and friendliness and I am sure that they did not mean to be aggressive. They were probably surprised when they put visiting drivers into a state of panic because they had only a small space to squeeze through while the Cretan whizzed through as if in a Formula One Race.

Not long out of Plakias the road narrowed suddenly where a landslide had eaten well into it. There was no warning sign, nor any protective fencing. A van was approaching, its driver was obviously a Cretan. He may not have meant to be aggressive but he did give the impression that it was not for the local drivers to take evasive action in a situation like this so he approached us as though we did not exist. There was a precipitous drop on one side and loose stones from the landslide on the other. The Suzuki had no high tech equipment such as ejection systems and parachutes for take off over the precipice, so Alex chose not to take issue and eased over, unfortunately too late to see a large stone dislodged by a landslide projecting a little over the road edge.

We hit it a real smack and the front tyre was badly slashed. I don't know the Greek for the expletives that burst forth from Alex and I am certainly not going to write it in English. The Ballater Eagle would put its wings over its ears. The spare tyre was smaller than the other tyres. It seems daft but apparently it was only intended only for an emergency and had to be replaced as soon as possible. We headed back to Plakias and the hirer gave us a replacement car, a Fiesta. I forbore to say to Alex that he should ask for a Mercedes.

We had no more incidents and actually we had a super first day getting to know the restaurants, the tavernas and the quality of the local wine, not a matter to be undertaken too hastily

Once we felt reasonably at home with traversing the mountain roads in the Fiesta, we set out for Sphakia to take a trip down memory lane. It was during the Battle of Crete that most of the gaps in my memory occurred.

I was stationed at Canea, a town on the north coast of Crete, when the order came for all Allied troops to withdraw to Sphakia, a small fishing village about 40 miles away on the South Coast. The Royal Navy was attempting another Dunkirk, an evacuation of thousands of troops in the face of a vastly superior Air Force. This time there was little or no RAF to assist the evacuation so the Navy was under constant bombardment and could only come in to the beaches at night.

The road from Canea to Sphakia was really just a very steep track winding its way through the White Mountains. The highest mountain in the range is over 7500 feet. Transport was not available so the troops, many thousands strong, had to walk. The intense heat of a Cretan summer and the lack of food and water meant that many succumbed to the horrendous conditions. The pace was very slow so it was necessary to conduct rearguard actions to hold the Germans back and allow as many troops as possible to be evacuated.

I took part in the last two rearguard actions. The first was in the plain of Askifou up in the mountains, the second and last was near Imvros Gorge, a short distance from Sphakia. On the last night of the evacuation we were withdrawn to a spot just above Sphakia. Unfortunately we were left behind, the island was surrendered and we were taken prisoners of war.

After such a long time I was a bit vague on some of the details of that event and I hoped that a visit to Sphakia might revive some lost memories. As we left Plakias and headed up into the mountains you can imagine how many thoughts were flooding through my mind. (I don't mean puncturing the tyre on that large stone!)

It was very probable that the environment of 1941 would now be changed out of all recognition. After all, 58 years is a long time. As we approached Sphakia I knew immediately that my search there would be fruitless. Sphakia was a thriving tourist centre. New houses covered the hillside and the bay was full of restaurants and shops from end to end.

We walked out to the point of a long pier and scanned the hillside above the village but nothing I saw raised any memories. I could not confirm the spot where I was left behind. We visited a lovely memorial that had been erected to commemorate the evacuation. It was on a beautiful site, at the edge of the seafront with the blue Libyan Sea as a background, such a peaceful scene. I looked around the busy and colourful village of Sphakia and thought how time can change things. I wondered whether any ghosts of that same scene in 1941 were now at peace.

We decided to have a meal at a seaside restaurant and then venture into the mountains to try to identify the places where the rearguard action took place. The owner of the restaurant found out that I was a veteran of the Battle of Crete and we were given marvellous attention and, paradise for a Scot, another free dram. I had been told that the

Sphakia - Coastline looking west.

Photograph by Alex Sinclair

War Memorial for 1941 evacuation.

Photograph by Alex Sinclair

memory of the Battle was considered an important part of Crete's history and is commemorated every year. I was surprised, however, how enthusiastic everyone was to meet a veteran of that battle.

Hopefully I would begin to recall some incidents long forgotten or at least confirm that my memories of incidents that I did recall were reasonably accurate. As we climbed into the hills my memory of the narrow and steep hairpin bends and the depth of the Imvros Gorge was confirmed. I was also able to correct my description of the actual site of the final rearguard action.

One mystery that puzzled me was not solved. In 1941 I was involved in the last rearguard action at the upper end of the Imvros. There was a village nearby called Vitrolokoumos. In a book on the Battle of Crete, there was a sketch of the road from Canea to Sphakia and Vitrolokoumos was on that sketch. Alex and I went over that whole area and there was no sign of any village in the area. Alex thought that the Imvros Gorge was so steep that it would seem an unlikely place for a rearguard action. We asked a good number of Cretans but nobody had heard of a village of that name or any village near it that might have been renamed.

If any villagers were suspected of harbouring the Resistance fighters the German forces would wreak terrible revenge. On occasions they would annihilate the whole village. Perhaps Vitrolokoumos met this awful fate.

I used a computer to write this book and I am reminded of a facility for moving a piece of text from one place to another. To activate this action you press a button called 'Cut'. You then select the place to which you want it moved and press another button called 'Paste'. Hey presto, by magic the text reappears. I wonder if a real live enactment of that disaster occurred and the Germans pressed the 'Cut' button on Vitrolokoumos and the 'Paste' button will forever remain unpressed.

We climbed further into the mountains until we reached the Plain of Askifou where the penultimate rearguard action occurred. Although I recognised the configuration of the Plain of Askifou the whole

Imvros Gorge

Photograph by Alex Sinclair

environment had developed out of all recognition. However, as we passed through the little village of Askifou Alex espied a notice that stated simply 'Museum'. It was not a fancy commercial notice but was written in the same way that you would write 'Wet Paint'. We decided to give it a quick visit. Another hand-painted notice on the wall of a small house was even less impressive. It turned out to be one of the most interesting episodes of our researches and one that brought back many memories.

The space in front of the house was covered in military artefacts, British, German and Cretan, helmets, rifles and machine guns. A wee wizened elderly wifie came forward. Was this the Curator? She was in the familiar black clothes worn by elderly Cretan women but her smile was warm and friendly.

Our knowledge of Greek was on a par with her knowledge of English so body language and mimicry played a major part in our communication. We were ushered into a large room that served as the museum. The wall was covered in photographs of British and German troops and of the local resistance groups. I gathered that her husband had fought with the resistance but I was not sure because she did not look old enough.

All manner of guns, from the old 1914 British Lee-Enfield rifle, that had been my basic issue, to the German Spandau machine gun of 1941. Photo albums and magazines relating to the Battle of Crete were also very interesting to me, I could have used some of them in my book. The old lady indicated that all the artefacts were dug up from the area around Askifou.

Alex managed to convey to the old lady that I was involved in the rearguard on Askifou Plain. She was quite excited and, as I mentioned earlier, when a veteran from Britain is recognised, the wee drams of ouzo were produced with the very sweet pastries that the Cretans love. I was shown family photographs but the sign language was hard-pushed to follow the family relationships.

Just before we left Alex spotted an old rusty Lewis gun, similar to the one that I had at the rearguard at Askifou. He tried to convey this to our hostess by pointing to the gun and then to me and pretended to fire it. For a moment she looked apprehensive and I thought that she was afraid that I was going to claim it as mine. As we bade goodbye to the gentle old lady, I was ever so grateful that Alex had spotted her home-made notice.

The last area to be visited on our research trail, on one of the few wet days of our holiday, was the capital town of Canea. It had expanded beyond all recognition. If I found it difficult to trace sites in the little village of Sphakia, I had absolutely no hope of tracing anything here and I soon gave up the idea.

In 1941 we had been so concerned in preparing for the German invasion that our movements were very restricted, so I had no idea that Canea was such fascinating place. The ambience, the goods in the shops, the narrow streets and the varied architecture, particularly the old harbour, all showed the influence of many cultures down through the ages. We spent some interesting hours there.

Author at Askifou Museum'

Photograph by Alex Sinclair

A sad moment of the holiday was the visit to Suda Bay Military Cemetery where those of the Allied Forces killed in the Battle of Crete are buried. The grounds, in a beautiful setting, are kept in marvellous condition. The grass is immaculate. All the gravestones face West up Suda Bay towards the sea. On the Southern arm of the Bay a range of mountains rise high into the sky, forming a magnificent backdrop.

May is the best month of the year to see the amazing variety of plants on Crete in full bloom and I think most of them were represented here. Every grave had its own plant and the blaze of colour was stunning.

I was not aware that so many young men had lost their lives in the Battle of Crete. There were almost 1000 graves. I was deeply moved as I stood by those of some members of the Royal Marines.

Each gravestone is of the same design, with letters of the same format identifying the Regiment, the Home Station (Chatham, Portsmouth, etc.), and the name of the Marine. Sadly, there were some exceptions to that format. The identity of many Marines was unknown and the engraving on their gravestones was brief and poignant: 'Known to God'.

The inability to identify their bodies was testimony to the intensity of the devastating bombing in those awful weeks of May 1941. It brought back vivid memories. My thoughts went out to the many parents who had lost their sons, still in their early 20's, and who would not be at rest until they saw their graves. It would have been terrible for any parents who could not find a gravestone with their son's name on it. As they looked down the lines they must have felt a great sadness not to know whether their boy was actually under one of those headstones, marked 'Known to God'.

I stood beside the graves and looked out over Suda Bay, thinking what a big part that strip of water had played in our lives in 1941. We had sailed into the bay to join the other forces in the abortive attempt to halt the German invasion. A few weeks later we sailed out again, en route for a four year spell in a German POW camp. Conditions were

Suda Bay Cemetery where there are around 1,000 graves of Royal Marines. The Author pays his respects to his comrades.

Photograph by Alex Sinclair

dreadful, the future uncertain and we all felt that fate had given us a raw deal.

Now I was acutely aware that the hundreds of lads lying under those gravestones facing Suda Bay had had no future to face. If only they could have lived to sail away with us. Although many years had rolled by and I was now old, I could still see the faces, forever young in my mind, of my former comrades.

The remainder of our holiday was devoted to exploring the hills around the south coast. Leaving the busy coastal resorts and going up into the hills is like entering another world. The population is sparse, the villages small and widely dispersed, but no matter how small each village has its Taverna, a place where you can have a drink and something to eat. You could hardly call it a pub, in some cases it was just a small room.

The locals, mainly elderly, sat around drinking and playing board games. You were always made very welcome. There was the usual language barrier but a mutual liking for the local wines helped overcome that and we had many interesting exchanges.

On one occasion we planned a walk into the hills where, according to the map, there was a track leading to a village. The prospect of lunch at the inevitable Taverna provided the motivation for me to make it up to the top of the steep climb on that hot day.

Alex was in his element. He has a keen interest in wildflowers and the hills on Crete in May are festooned with masses of them. If we came across an unusual specimen, he would bend down with his bottom skywards and focus his camera on it. Even if only a puff of wind was blowing, he would stay transfixed until the flower stopped vibrating. Sometimes I thought he had fallen asleep but I dared not touch him. The profusion of flowers was astounding. At one point a bank many feet wide of bright yellow flowers spilled down from the edge of the track broadening by several yards by the time it reached the bottom of the hill, resembling a flow of molten lava from a volcano.

When I wrote about the steep hills and the tremendous heat in May and June, I thought that perhaps my memory had played tricks. This walk confirmed that I had not exaggerated when I said that my body had cried out for a halt and for water on these roads so long ago and I tried just to look ahead and to keep my mind on positive thoughts.

Although the conditions now were very different from those in 1941, I began to feel very hot and my old legs were aching a bit as I plodded up the hill behind Alex. I recalled in a light-hearted way that I should once more look ahead and keep my mind on positive thoughts but this time only as far as the Taverna up the hill and of Alex and I sipping a nice cold glass of wine.

We progressed well up into the hills but the maps of Crete are not very dependable and we found ourselves in doubt about advancing further. Alex did a reconnaissance climb to the top of the hill and thought we could take a chance on that route. But he changed his mind because, I suspect, I must have looked as I felt, knackered. Eventually we had to double back but we did reach the village and we did have our bottle of wine. Mission accomplished

The remaining days passed very pleasantly and the holiday came all too soon to an end. On our way to the airport Alex stopped to take some more photographs of the cemetery because the light had been poor on the first visit. As we prepared to depart, several very large cars drew up at the gates with an impressive entourage in tow. I recognised the uniforms of the German Army and the brass on one of them indicated a high rank.

The irony of the situation struck me. Here was I, a veteran of the Battle of Crete, quietly paying my last respects when a host of German soldiers descended on the place. We were both taken aback. The last time I had stood at Suda Bay was when I was being transported from Crete to Germany as a POW, a German soldier had prodded me with a rifle, yelling at me to move on. It was unlikely that the one with all the Brass would prod me in the back and shout at me but I decided once more just to move on.

It transpired that this was an official visit of a German General accompanied by the German Ambassador in Greece and a large party. Alex felt that it would do them good to be introduced to a veteran of the Battle of Crete and hear at first hand what it was all about. The next thing that I knew there was a young German Captain approaching me as I stood beside the graves of the Marines.

The bold Alex had marched over and spoken to the party. The Officer was polite and expressed himself in very appreciative terms of the great and sad loss of life. I am sure that he was sincere but I was glad to walk away, an ironic end to my trip down memory lane, wasn't it?

Suda Bay War Memorial

Photograph by Alex Sinclair

Acknowledgements

I would like to thank Alex Sinclair, Mary and Gillespie Munro, Sabine Muir, Librarian and the staff at the Ballater Library, and also the many friends who have helped me and encouraged me to write this book.

I especially mention Alex Sinclair who tackled my drafts so assiduously. I spent many a pleasant evening while Alex, pulling no punches but with characteristic diplomacy, plied me with so many points of structure, grammar and accuracy that I recalled schooldays when the English Master exhausted his red ink pen on my essays. The main difference was that the Master was not so diplomatic and did not soften the lesson with drams of Laphroaig whisky.

I also thank Alex for accompanying me to Crete when we traversed the 'Via Dolorosa' in 1998 to see whether it would bring back memories to fill the gaps in my story of that march. I describe that visit at Appendix G. Though filled with sad memories, a real compensation was to see the beauties of that lovely island in peacetime, and to enjoy again the friendship of the Cretans. We celebrated my 78th birthday there so I repaid Alex's Laphroaig with interest. I am grateful to Alex for the photographs he took of scenes in Crete that are included in the book. Alex also took the photograph of me on the back cover.

Unless you are very famous, the world of publishing is a forbidding jungle to unknown authors. It is difficult to persuade publishers even to read your manuscript. So I thank Sabine Muir, librarian, and the founder and leader of the Ballater Writers Group, for encouraging me and helping me to penetrate that jungle. At the time of writing, Sabine is the Editor of the Ballater Eagle. Angus Brown was the Writer in Residence for Aberdeenshire County Council. He considered that one of his main tasks was to set up a series of projects aimed at publishing the work of new writers, a much needed facility. I wish him good luck in his projects. He gave me invaluable advice for which I am grateful.

I emphasised in the book my ignorance of the planning and strategy of the Battle of Crete and told how much that lack of information had affected us. So I read with immense interest Antony Beevor's book about the Battle of Crete, The Battle and the Resistance. I admired the detailed documentation and historical information and was over-awed by the amount of research that he must have undertaken. As I read his analysis of situations in which I was involved, I relived and re-assessed many of these events with a completely different perspective. I acknowledge with thanks that I have been able to insert at Appendix E the Ultra signal to General Freyberg. I was intrigued by Mr Beevor's theory of the effect that the General's interpretation of the signal might have had on his decision about the main thrust of the German invasion.

I also read with great interest Greece and Crete by the historian Christopher Buckley, written at the request of HM Government. I learned much that was not known to me at the time and have received approval from the publishers, Her Majesty' Stationery Office, to insert at Appendix F a few pages relating to the period of the march over the mountains to Sphakia and the rearguard actions in which I was involved. I acknowledge with thanks that 'Crown copyright is produced with permission of the Controller of Her Majesty's Stationery Office.'

I acknowledge with thanks the photographs of the Battle of Crete provided by the Trustees of the Imperial War Museum.

I record my appreciation of the efforts, unfortunately without success, of the New Zealand War Archives Museum to trace the sources of photographs in the New Zealand film of the Battle of Crete, Touch and Go.

The Mitchell Library in Glasgow holds on microfilm copies of editions of newspapers published in Glasgow for many years back. They tried hard to trace the edition of the Glasgow evening paper that carried the article about my capture under the heading, "Crete Hero Missing". They hold only one edition for each day and as they could not trace the article, they decided that it must have been in an extra edition. My thanks to them for their efforts.

In Appendix A I have acknowledged my use of the title of John Brown's book, *In Durance Vile*, as the heading of Part 3 of this book. I also referred to one or two incidents from John's book. I attempted to seek approval for the foregoing by contacting Nan Brown, John's wife, whose name appears on the flyleaf of the book as the publisher but she was not known at the address that John gave me. As a matter of courtesy I contacted Robert Hale, the firm mentioned in the flyleaf beneath Nan Brown's name. They did not know to whom I should apply for approval.

The countless vain attempts to persuade mainstream publishers even to look at this book severely blunted my enthusiasm. Regardless of the quality of a book, the reply was always - 'memoirs are only acceptable when the author is famous'. This relates even more especially to war memoirs. So I was heartened to find on the Internet a new technique that is revolutionising the publishing world.

A printing technology has now been developed that can deliver a soft-back book in as little 72 hours. The practice of printing books when they are ordered, or 'Print-on-Demand' as it is called, has dispensed with the need for expensive print runs and book storage, making non–commercial titles viable to publish. The book is placed on the Internet and can be ordered from anywhere in the world.

Thus I have decided to have 'Almost a Hero' published by a new firm here in Scotland, Gopher UK, who have access to the latest internet 'Print on Demand' techniques.

Thanks to my sons, Alistair and Brian for helping me to plough through the many aspects of the computer jungle.

About the Author

Alex Clark was born in Glasgow, Scotland, 1920. He entered the Civil Service in 1938 as a Sorting Clerk and Telegraphist and retired in 1978, having reached the rank of Principal in the General Register Office. He was called up to the Royal Marines in 1940 and fought in the Battle of Crete in 1941. He was involved in the last rearguard action, was one of thousands left behind when Crete was surrendered and spent the next four years as a POW in Germany. He rejoined the Marines in 1945, was training for the Far East but when the war ended in that area he returned to civilian life.

Alex is now retired and lives in the village of Ballater in the Highlands of Scotland. His main interests are writing, angling (founder President of the Ballater Angling Association), gardening, golf (Captain of the NE of Scotland Seniors Golf Association and Councillor of the Royal Burgess Golfing Club, the 2nd oldest golf club in the world). Now that he is a retired widower living alone, perhaps, somewhat regrettably, he must add housework.

Alex has written many short stories and articles which have appeared in local papers. As founder president he undertook to write a book about the Angling Association's activities on the River Dee, the world famous salmon river on Royal Deeside. The book, called 'The Happy Fishers', was published in 1996 and is on the Amazon web site.

Editing:	Judith Hampson
Cover Design:	Digital Canvas
Layout:	Stephen Young
Font:	Adobe Garamond (11pt)